CAREERS

in

Healthcare

Management

HOW TO FIND YOUR
PATH AND FOLLOW IT

Cynthia Carter Haddock,
Robert A. McLean, and
Robert C. Chapman

Health Administration Press
Chicago, Illinois

Your board, staff, or clients may also benefit from this book's insight. For more information on quantity discounts, contact the Health Administration Press Marketing Manager at (312) 424–9470.

06   05   04   03   02   5   4   3   2   1

Library of Congress Cataloging-in-Publication Data

Haddock, Cynthia Carter
    Careers in healthcare management : how to find your path and follow it / by Cynthia Carter Haddock, Robert A. McLean, Robert C. Chapman.
        p. cm.
    Includes bibliographical references.
    ISBN 1-56793-174-X (alk. paper)
        1. Medicine—Vocational guidance—Miscellanea. 2. Health services administration. 3. McLean, Robert A. I. Chapman, Robert C., FACHE. II. Title

    R690 .H334 2002
    353.6'023—dc21   2001051751

The paper used in this publication meets the minimum requirements of American National Standard for Information Sciences—Permanence of Paper for Printed Library Materials, ANSI Z39.48–1984. (TM)

Acquisitions editor: Marcy McKay; Project manager: Cami Cacciatore; Cover and text design: Matt Avery

Health Administration Press
A division of the Foundation of the

American College of Healthcare Executives
1 North Franklin Street, Suite 1700
Chicago, IL 60606–3491
(312) 424–2800

For my parents, Charles and Gloria Carter,
and for my daughter Elizabeth
—*Cynthia Carter Haddock*

For my mother, Alice McLean,
for my wife, Sharon,
and for my sons Rob and Scott
—*Robert A. McLean*

For my parents, Curtis and Roberta Chapman,
and for my wife June
—*Robert C. Chapman*

CONTENTS

Preface

IN MANY YEARS of healthcare management practice and education, we have often faced difficult questions from students and early careerists:

- What do healthcare managers do?
- How can I prepare for a career in healthcare management?
- How can I be a healthcare manager if I am not a doctor (or nurse or other healthcare provider)?
- What is the difference between healthcare management and hospital administration?
- Is healthcare management really substantively different from other managerial endeavors?
- Which is "better," an MBA or an MHA (or a JD or an MPH)?
- What is the best way to begin my career in healthcare management?

Some of these questions are profound, and some reflect profound confusion. Misinformation about careers in healthcare management is at least as abundant as good information.

The field of healthcare management offers unique challenges and rewards, both emotional and financial. It remains, however, a field few understand and even fewer set out to pursue. We wanted to explain the rewards and encourage outstanding new talent to pursue them. To provide answers to those difficult questions, we began to prepare this book.

To find out what healthcare managers do, and how they prepared for their careers, we decided to ask them. We asked a sample of university-based healthcare management programs, both undergraduate and graduate, and a few professional organizations for the names of exemplary managers and executives from among their alumni and memberships. From the names we received, we surveyed a sample of individuals representing a broad range of specializations, industry segments, and career stages. The 51 profiles included here are the responses to our survey.

We explored the following questions with each person in our sample:

- Why did you decide to enter the field?
- How did you prepare for your career?
- What career path have you taken?
- What are your current duties and responsibilities?
- What advice would you give to someone beginning their career in healthcare management?

We were especially pleased by the thoughtful responses we received, all of which are included here.

Part One of the book provides some background information. Chapter 1 offers a brief of the history of the healthcare management profession and of its graduate programs.

Chapter 2 focuses on educational preparation for healthcare management careers and gives suggestions to those looking for a graduate program in which to enroll. Chapter 3 explores the labor market environment in which managers' employment and compensation are determined. It also shows that both current compensation levels and prospects for the near future are excellent. Chapter 4 provides career and professional development advice for those beginning their careers in the field. Part II includes 51 profiles, and the appendix provides contact information for several of the professional associations of interest to new entrants.

This book will be helpful to several groups of readers. It offers early careerists insights into the field as it shows how winding, yet fulfilling, a career path can be. We hope it will inspire them to seek out mentors, be mentors themselves, take professional risks, and be lifelong learners.

Those who are considering careers in healthcare management will also benefit from this book. Important lessons can be learned from the experiences of successful managers and executives in the field. Each of our contributors has provided advice, and their collective wisdom will help the next generation of healthcare managers start off on the right foot.

Teachers and advisers to students and prospective students of healthcare management will find this book useful in answering the questions that have vexed instructors over the years. New students enter the field each year, and their questions deserve thoughtful and complete answers.

Finally, practicing healthcare managers may also find this a valuable resource. Leaders in healthcare management, perhaps more than those in most managerial fields, take seriously the responsibility to mentor novices and to develop new talent.

Preparing the book has been complicated by our own career progressions. When we began, all of us lived and worked in Birmingham, Alabama. As we finish, we are in three widely separated cities. That we have kept, more or less, to our schedule is testimony to the pleasure we have had in this effort.

Our deepest thanks go to our colleagues and contributors, who have shared their professional stories with us. Our warmest wishes go to those who will read and benefit from these stories.

PART ONE

CHAPTER ONE

A Brief History of Healthcare Management

IN MANY WAYS, healthcare management is a "hidden" career. When we think of a hospital or a clinic, we tend to think of physicians, nurses, and other caregivers. The myriad of people who work in the organizations that support health services delivery organizations, like insurance and managed care companies and government policy-making and regulatory agencies, are even more invisible and are not who we think of when we hear the phrase "health services." However, they play very important roles in making health services available and accessible.

Think of medical dramas on television or in the movies. Rarely do you see a health services executive among the characters, and when you do, it is many times in a rather unflattering light, such as the greedy executive who is more concerned about money than patients. The news media also tend to focus on hands-on caregivers in health services organizations or to present executives in these organizations negatively.

This book will help you see the range of work options that are available to health services executives. It will also help you see that careers in this field take many different directions and many different paths. Most of all, we hope that this book will help you see the incredibly important role that healthcare executives play in health services delivery in the United States. While these executives may often be hidden and work behind the scenes, they have a tremendous effect on the availability, accessibility, and quality of health services in our communities. They help to provide an environment in which physicians, nurses, and other caregivers can practice effectively and efficiently, and they help provide safe, comfortable, and compassionate places for people to receive health services when needed. Although they are concerned about the business side of healthcare, ultimately they are concerned about the health of people in the communities they serve.

There is not one term for the field we are talking about or the people who practice it—healthcare management, health services administration, and other variants can be used interchangeably. People who practice in this field may be called health services executives, healthcare administrators, health services managers, or other similar names. This can be confusing if you are new to healthcare, but it will become second nature. Another source of confusion is the fact that administrators may be identified by the specific type of organization in which they work, for example, as a hospital executive or nursing home administrator. However, the meaning of such terms is usually clear.

The development of healthcare management as a career field has largely followed the development of medical science and the growth of hospitals in the United States. Until the early part of the twentieth century, very little could actually be done in hospitals to improve the health of patients. People who had enough money received nursing care in their homes when they were ill or dying or having a child. Those who became hospital patients were generally poor and without family or friends to care for them. However, with the advent of antisepsis and anesthesia, the development of modern surgery, and the discovery of antibiotics in the late 1800s and early 1900s, hospitals became places that could offer cures and relieve suffering. Between 1875 and 1925, the number of hospitals in the United States grew from just over 170 to about 7,000, and the number of hospital beds increased from 35,000 to 860,000 (Rosner 1989).

Early hospital administrators were called "superintendents" and typically had little specific training for their jobs—many were nurses who had taken on administrative responsibilities. Over half of the superintendents who belonged to the American Hospital Association in 1916 were graduate nurses, and the first formal hospital administration and nursing school administration educational program, in health economics, was established for nurses at Columbia Teachers College in New York in 1900 (Stevens 1999). Other hospital superintendents were physicians, laypersons, and Catholic sisters.

The first degree-granting program in hospital administration was established at Marquette University in Wisconsin. The original idea for this program came from Father Moulinier, a force behind the Catholic Hospital Association and a member of the 1922 Rockefeller Commission on the Training of Hospital Executives. In 1927, two students, both women religious, received their degrees, but by 1928, the program, with no other graduates, had failed (Neuhauser 1983).

In 1929, Michael Davis published his book *Hospital Administration, A Career: The Need for Trained Executives for a Billion Dollar Business, and How They May Be Trained*, proposing a two-year graduate degree curriculum in hospital administration. The first year of this curriculum was centered on coursework in accounting, statistics, management, economics and the social sciences, and the history of hospitals and the health professions, with limited practical observation. The second year was mostly spent in practical work with some coursework in business policy, public health, and labor relations.

Following on Davis' proposal for graduate training in hospital administration, the Committee on the Costs of Medical Care in October 1932 stated:

> Hospitals and clinics are not only medical institutions, they are also social and business enterprises, sometimes very large ones. It is important, therefore, that they be directed by administrators who are trained for their responsibilities and can understand and integrate the various professional, economic, and social factors involved. Definite opportunities should be provided in universities or in institutes of hospital administration connected with universities, for the theoretical and practical training of such administrators. The administration of hospitals and medical centers should be developed as a career which will attract high-grade students.

However, before the founding of the first graduate program in hospital administration, a group of practicing administrators came together in 1933 to form the American College of Hospital Administrators (now the American College of Healthcare Executives), the first professional association for hospital administrators. And, while both clinically trained and lay administrators could affiliate with the new College, the emphasis was clearly on the lay administrator. Among the 106 charter fellows of the College, 16 were women and 32 were physicians (Stevens 1999).

The professional status of the field was furthered in 1934 when the University of Chicago established the first graduate program in hospital administration, naming Michael Davis as its head. The new program was largely based on the model that Davis had proposed a few years earlier. In the 1940s, eight new university graduate programs in health administration joined the Chicago program, nine more followed in the 1950s, with 15 more in the 1960s. Many of these programs followed the Davis model of one year of coursework and one year of practical experience. In 1958, the Sloan graduate program in hospital administration at Cornell University in New York started a new trend toward a two-year graduate program, a model that is followed by most programs today (Stevens 1999). The early programs used the term "hospital administration" in their titles; however, this, too, has changed to "healthcare administration" or some similar phrase, as the field has changed to include a broader range of organizations in which healthcare executives work.

Just as the American College of Hospital Administrators modified its name to the American College of Healthcare Executives (ACHE) a number of years ago to reflect the wider range of organizations in which administrators worked, other professional associations have undergone name changes, reflective of the changing nature of the field and employment opportunities. The National Association of Clinic Managers, founded in 1926, changed its name to the Medical Group Management Association (MGMA) in 1963. The American Association of Hospital Accountants, established in 1946, changed its name to the Hospital Financial Management Association in 1968 and then changed its name again, in 1982, to the Healthcare Financial Management Association (HFMA).

The number of academic programs for healthcare executives has grown over the years, and the programs have organized to continue to improve the quality of health administration education. In 1948, several early graduate programs in the field joined together to form the Association of University Programs in Health Administration (AUPHA). This association now includes both graduate and undergraduate health administration programs and focuses its efforts on the development and continuous improvement of health management education.

In 1968, the Accrediting Commission on Graduate Education for Hospital Administration was incorporated as the accrediting agency for graduate programs in health administration. The name of this accrediting body was changed in 1976 to the Accrediting Commission on Education for Health Services Administration (ACEHSA). Today, ACEHSA is sponsored by a group of educational and professional associations (including the American College of Healthcare Executives, the American College of Medical Practice Executives, the American Hospital Association, the American Public Health Association, the Association of University Programs in Health Administration, the Blue Cross Blue Shield Association, the Canadian College of Health Services Executives, the Healthcare Financial Management Association, the Health Information Management and Systems Society, and the Health Insurance Association of America) devoted to accountability and quality improvement in the education of health administration professionals and serves as the recognized accrediting body for master's programs in health administration in the United States and Canada.

Over the course of the last century, the field of healthcare administration and the organizations in which executives work have changed dramatically. Hospitals have become large, complex organizations; technology has advanced at an almost unbelievable rate; the financing of healthcare has moved from self-pay to a complicated third-party reimbursement system; and government has taken an increasingly larger role in healthcare delivery (Rosenberg 1987). Despite these increased complications, the field continues to sustain three primary objectives.

First, healthcare administrators are responsible for the business and financial aspects of hospitals, clinics, and other health services organizations, and are focused on increasing efficiency and financial stability. Their roles include human resources management, financial management, cost accounting, data collection and analysis, strategic planning, marketing, and the various maintenance functions of the organization. Second, healthcare administrators are responsible for providing the most basic social service: the care of dependent people at the most vulnerable points in their lives. Third, healthcare administrators are responsible for maintaining the moral and social order of their organizations, serving as advocates for patients, arbitrators in situations where there are competing values, and intermediaries for the various professional groups who practice within the organization. As healthcare services have become increasingly expensive and as the environment for the organizations that deliver these services has become more turbulent and hostile, these three objectives seem more and more contradictory (Rosner 1989). However, the three objectives remain. The greatest challenge for health services executives and for the educational programs that train them is to find the skills and competencies needed to balance these objectives and to achieve them in a continuously changing environment.

Today, the opportunities for healthcare administrators are increasing and the challenges they face in ensuring effective, efficient healthcare services for communities are many. Shortages of nurses and other healthcare workers, concern for the safety and quality of healthcare services, rising costs, a growing number of uninsured Americans, an aging population, and rapidly changing medical technology and practice all make the field of health administration a very big job for those who are willing to accept the challenge. For those who do, the rewards come in knowing that you are making a positive difference in the lives of people and communities.

REFERENCES

Neuhauser, D. 1983. *Coming of Age*. Chicago: Pluribus Press.

Rosenberg, C.E. 1987. *The Care of Strangers*. New York: Basic Books.

Rosner, D. 1989. "Doing Well or Doing Good: The Ambivalent Focus of Hospital Administration." In *The American General Hospital: Communities and Social Contexts*, edited by D. Long and J. Golden, 157–169. Ithaca, New York: Cornell University Press.

Stevens, R. 1999. *In Sickness and in Wealth: American Hospitals in the Twentieth Century.* Baltimore: The Johns Hopkins University Press.

CHAPTER TWO

Educational Preparation

WITH THE EXCEPTION of nursing home administrators, most healthcare executives are not licensed. No test must be passed, and no minimum credentials must be obtained; therefore, no one standard educational entry point to a career in this field exists. Healthcare management careers can begin with a variety of educational backgrounds. In this chapter, we discuss undergraduate and graduate programs in health administration, recognizing that other educational options exist.

The question of whether or not healthcare administration is a unique management activity that requires specialized training specific to the field has been debated for a number of years. In 1954, Herluf Olson, former Dean of the School of Business at Dartmouth College, undertook one of the earliest examinations of this question. Olson began his study believing that hospital administration was not a unique management activity. After closely studying the field, however, he changed his opinion and recognized that hospital administration deserved a specialized course of study. He attributed the field's uniqueness to the very unusual organizational structure of hospitals, the distinctiveness of the medical staff as an organizational form, a financing mechanism (third-party payment) totally different from other organizations, and the fact that the guiding ethic of the hospital was community welfare as opposed to corporate well-being.

While the debate still continues with no clear resolution, the characteristics Olson cited remain unchanged. We believe that specialized education in health services administration has merit and should be seriously considered by anyone exploring a career as a healthcare executive.

UNDERGRADUATE PROGRAMS

Undergraduate programs in health administration have existed since the mid- to late-1960s in many different kinds of educational institutions—small colleges, large universities, public and private institutions. These full-time and part-time programs exist in a variety of academic departments and schools, including business, political science, nursing, community health, and allied health.

A mark of quality and professional recognition for undergraduate health administration programs is full membership in the Association of University Programs in Health Administration (AUPHA). Such membership indicates that the program has voluntarily submitted to a review by faculty from peer programs and has successfully met a set of criteria established by AUPHA as measures of quality education. Programs maintain their full membership status through periodic reviews and continuous improvement. Developing programs and those working toward full membership may be associate members of AUPHA. A list of all full and associate member programs can be obtained from AUPHA (see the appendix for contact information).

Many students who complete undergraduate degrees in health administration will also go on to complete graduate degrees in the field. Others will directly enter healthcare administration careers in hospitals, long-term care facilities, physician practices, or other types of health services organizations.

GRADUATE PROGRAMS

A master's degree is the terminal professional educational credential for people entering health services management. Different from other fields like business (where an MBA is the recognized degree) or medicine (where the MD is the recognized credential), there is not one degree title that is used in health administration. And, although only schools of business offer the MBA and only schools of medicine offer the MD, there is not one university home for graduate programs in health administration.

Health administration degrees may be found with many titles, including MHA (Master of Health Administration), MHSA (Master of Health Services Administration), or MSHA (Master of Science in Health Administration), among others. Graduate health administration programs may also offer the MBA (Master of Business Administration) or MPH (Master of Public Health) with health administration concentrations. Such programs can be found in schools of business, public health, allied health, and medicine; however, most are in schools of business and public health. Some universities offer joint or dual degrees, such as combined degrees in health administration and law, medicine, business, or nursing. These combined programs offer students the ability to obtain multiple educational credentials, typically in a shorter period of time than if both degrees were pursued separately.

Accreditation

Graduate programs in health administration are accredited by the Accrediting Commission on Education for Health Services Administration (ACEHSA), a body composed of representatives of various educational and professional associations in the field. Accreditation is a voluntary peer review process used as a means to improve the quality of graduate education in the health services administration. Approximately 70 programs in the U.S. and Canada are currently accredited by ACEHSA. A listing of these programs can be obtained from ACEHSA (see the appendix for contact information). Schools, as well as universities, in which health administration programs are located, may also be accredited. For example, the Council on Education for Public Health (CEPH) accredits schools of public health and The International Association of Management Education (AACSB) accredits schools of business. (You can find more information about AACSB and

CEPH in the appendix at the end of this book.) When reading that an educational program is accredited, it is helpful to distinguish whether the accreditation is at the program, school, or university level.

Although accredited health services administration programs can be quite variable in their university locations and degree titles and in the approach they take to graduate education, all accredited programs share some commonalities in their curricula. Curriculum content in ten areas is required as basic knowledge, understanding, skills, and values relevant to health services management:

1. structuring, marketing, and positioning health organizations to achieve optimum performance;
2. financial management of health organizations under alternative financing mechanisms;
3. leadership, interpersonal, and communication skills in managing human resources and health professionals in diverse organizational environments;
4. managing information resources and collecting, analyzing, and using business and health information in decision making;
5. statistical, quantitative, and economic analysis for decision making;
6. legal and ethical analysis applied to business and clinical decision making;
7. organizational and governmental health policy formulation, implementation, and effect;
8. assessment and understanding of the health status of populations, determinants of health and illness, and managing health risks and behaviors in diverse populations;
9. the development, organization, financing, performance, and change of health systems in diverse communities drawing broadly on the social and behavioral sciences; and
10. business and health outcomes measurement, process/outcome relationships, and methods for process improvement in health organizations.

Program Structure

As mentioned previously, early health administration programs were two years in length: one year of primarily academics and one year of primarily observation and practice. While graduate programs continue to be two years (or the equivalent) in length, both years are focused on coursework. However, graduate health administration programs continue to have a strong fieldwork or experiential component, combining academic coursework with applied work in healthcare organizations. This fieldwork component distinguishes graduate professional education from other types of graduate programs.

Fieldwork may take a number of forms in graduate programs. It may include course projects done in "real world" settings. It may also include relatively short (e.g., three months during the summer between the two years of coursework) periods of observation and practice in a healthcare organization, typically called internships. Longer (9 to 12 months) periods of practice, called residencies, may also be part of the degree program. Both internships and residencies are usually paid experiences for which students receive course credit and therefore also pay tuition. These fieldwork experiences are valuable and important parts of health administration education.

Health administration programs may be organized in one of several different formats. Some programs require full-time study, while others can be completed on a part-time basis. Other programs are presented in an executive format, designed to meet the needs of practicing healthcare executives by meeting on weekends or for limited, but intense, periods of study (e.g., several weeks spaced throughout the year). Executive programs may also use a form of distance education as one component of the course of study. Some universities offer programs that use distance education exclusively, requiring no time on campus.

Selecting a Program

Selecting a graduate program is one of the most important decisions you will make in your career as a health services executive. The program you select is where you will begin to build a foundation of skills and knowledge and to develop a network of professional colleagues in health administration. When looking at graduate programs, explore the following:

- Is the program accredited? If so, by what accrediting body? If not, why not? Are the school and university in which the program is located accredited?
- What are the admission requirements of the program? Is there a preference or requirement for any specific educational preparation (e.g., undergraduate major or course prerequisites)? Is there an experience requirement? What is the minimum grade point average for admission? What standardized test scores are required?
- What does the curriculum look like? Is there a fieldwork component of the program? Are applied projects done in local healthcare organizations part of the program's coursework? If an internship or residency is required, is there placement help available?
- Does the program's structure meet your needs? For example, if you want to continue to work while completing your studies, is a part-time option available?
- What type of students does the program recruit? Are they diverse? What might they bring to the educational experience?
- What is the faculty like? Is there an adequate number of faculty members for the size of the student body? What is their educational preparation? Are they active researchers? Do they have good connections to the field of practice? Do any of the faculty members have experience as healthcare executives?
- Where do graduates of the program find employment? Does the program assist with placement? Are alumni actively involved with the program?
- What is the cost of the program? Is financial aid available?
- Do you feel comfortable in the university's setting (e.g., rural/ urban, public/private, small/large)? Would you feel comfortable living and learning there? Is it conducive to meeting your educational goals?

Many times applicants to programs consult the *U.S. News and World Report* ranking of graduate health administration programs. This ranking is based on results of surveys sent to deans, faculty, and administrators of accredited graduate programs. Respondents are asked to rate the academic quality of programs as distinguished (5 points), strong (4), good (3), adequate (2), or marginal (1), based on their own assessment of the quality of the curriculum, faculty, and graduates (respondents who are not familiar with a particular program may select "don't know" as a response). Scores for each program are then averaged across respondents who rated it. While these rankings can be used as one piece of information in making a decision, they should not be used as the only criterion in selecting a program. Reputational scores, even those based on the evaluation of people with a great deal of knowledge about the field, do not tell the whole story.

Selecting a graduate program requires gathering a great deal of information about the options available and also understanding your own strengths, areas that need improvement, and career aspirations. In addition to asking the questions above, you should, if possible, personally visit the program location. Ask to speak with students and faculty while you are there. Look at the classrooms, computer labs, libraries, and other facilities that will be available to you as a student. In addition, request to speak with one or more alumni of the program to hear what they have to say about their experiences as students, including how the program has contributed to their careers.

Ultimately, you should select a program that meets your needs and aspirations. It is also important that you select a program where you feel comfortable and believe you will be challenged and mentored in a way that will give you the best beginning for your career as a health services executive.

CONTINUING EDUCATION

Successful health executives must be lifelong learners. The information learned in a formal educational program will be quickly outdated as the healthcare field changes at an almost dizzying pace. In addition, you will need to hone and sharpen the skills you have and acquire new skills as you progress in your career, taking on new responsibilities and facing increasingly difficult challenges. Opportunities for continuing education are available in a variety of places. A number of graduate health administration programs also offer continuing education.

Professional associations provide many opportunities for continuing education throughout one's career (a list of healthcare administration professional associations can be found in the appendix at the end of this book). A number of these associations have voluntary certification programs for their members that provide evidence of an administrator's continued learning and skill acquisition.

For example, the American College of Healthcare Executives has three categories of affiliation: member, Diplomate, and Fellow. An affiliate who achieves Diplomate status must meet certain educational and experience requirements, have a specified number of continuing education hours in a given period of time, be active in community and civic activities, hold a management position in healthcare, and pass the Board of Governors Examination. This examination consists of 200 questions in 10 management areas and 30 questions regarding the College's *Code of Ethics*, by-laws, and regulations. The 10 management areas covered on the examination are:

1. governance and organization;
2. planning and marketing;
3. human resources;
4. financial and assets management;
5. plant and facility management;
6. healthcare information systems management;
7. quality assessment and improvement;
8. government regulations and law;
9. organizational arrangements and relationships; and
10. profession/education/research/ethics.

To achieve Fellow status, a Diplomate must have additional experience and continuing education and must complete a fellowship project. A person who is a Diplomate in College may use the letters CHE after his/her name, indicating that he/she is a Certified Healthcare Executive. Fellows of the College may use the letters FACHE (Fellow of the American College of Healthcare Executives) after their names. Other professional associations, such as the American College of Medical Practice Executives and the Healthcare Financial Management Association, have similar certification options, with fellowship being the highest level of certification.

SUMMARY

The healthcare environment changes rapidly and executives must be lifelong learners to keep up with these changes. A master's degree is the terminal educational credential for people entering the field of healthcare management and is a critically important starting point for your career. It provides a solid foundation for practice. However, your degree will be insufficient to sustain your progress, without continuing education and development throughout your career.

CHAPTER THREE

Careers and Labor Markets: The Matrix of Opportunities

OPPORTUNITIES FOR EMPLOYMENT, the path of career advancement, and compensation for professional efforts are determined in labor markets. A market is the set of arrangements, rules, norms, and institutions in which some good or service is purchased or sold. A labor market is the set of arrangements for matching workers with employers and for setting the price of labor, that is, the wage rate (Lehr, McLean, and Smith 1994).

Many labor markets are interrelated by the substitutability of one individual for another and by individuals' ability to move from one setting to another. These markets are defined along three dimensions: occupation, industry, and location, as depicted in Figure 3.1. Some individuals are closely tied to a particular occupation. An occupation is "what you do," a set of tasks that are similar from one employment setting to another. In general, the greater the educational qualifications for entry into an occupation, the greater are its members' attachments to it. Nurses, for example, display a greater attachment to their occupation than do salespeople. Medicine, dentistry, law, and, perhaps, healthcare management are examples of the extreme case, professions whose members display enormous occupational attachment.

Figure 3.1: The Matrix of Labor Market Opportunities

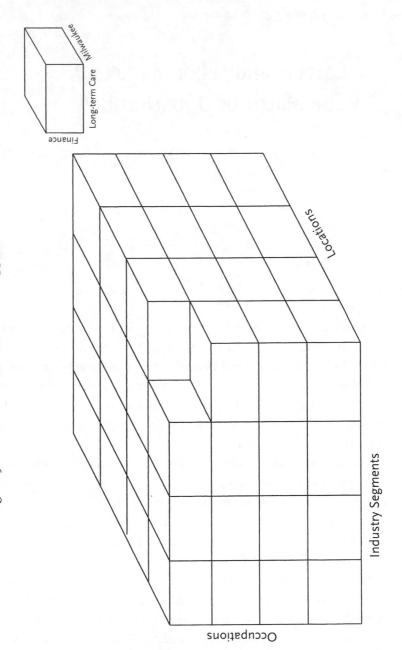

Some individuals are closely tied to an industry—a setting in which one works or a set of organizations that produce similar outputs. "Healthcare services" is a sector, which is a set of industries. Location refers to a geographic setting. Many individuals are tied, by tradition, family, or inertia to specific localities. Generally, as one's educational qualifications rise, and as the educational qualifications for one's occupation increase, one's ties to a specific location decrease.

The three-dimensional matrix shown in Figure 1 consists of a great many cells, each representing a specific occupation/industry/location combination. At any one time, a labor force participant holds a job in a single cell. Even the narrow world of healthcare management contains many such cells. Someone might, for example, be an operations manager (occupation) in an acute care hospital (industry) in Wichita Falls (location) or a financial manager (occupation) in a long-term care corporation (industry) headquartered in Milwaukee (location). "Healthcare" consists of many industries, and health administration consists of many occupations. Over the course of a career, one can occupy, successively, many of these cells.

Within each cell, the interaction of the supply of and the demand for employees' characteristics determines the compensation that an individual can expect. Some people believe that organizational rules or long tenure in office insulate them from the effect of supply and demand. In the long run, however, the internal labor market of an organization cannot be inconsistent with conditions in the external labor market, or the organization will experience shortages and other inefficiencies (Lehr, McLean, and Smith 1994).

MOBILITY AND THE MATRIX OF OPPORTUNITY

The three dimensions of the career matrix map the opportunities for career advancement in health services administration (or any other field of endeavor). Health services administration is not an industry, but a set of occupations. The U.S. Bureau of Labor Statistics publishes the *Dictionary of Occupational Titles* (U.S. Bureau of Labor Statistics 1991), listing the occupations in which the American workforce is currently engaged. Many such titles are held by health services administrators.

Occupation Number 187.117-010 is "Administrator, Healthcare Facility." That catch-all category includes a great many positions in the health administration field, but excludes such cross-over titles as director of security, director of information technology, and accountant. It also excludes such clinical management occupations as "Director, Nursing Services" (075.117-022) and "Director, Pharmacy Services" (074.167-010).

Simultaneously, healthcare encompasses a broad range of industries, as defined under the North American Industrial Classification System; some of these industries are quite widely separated in the coding system (see North American Industrial Classification System). For example, a single integrated healthcare system might include subsidiaries in industries as diverse as durable medical equipment sales (part of the retailing group), medical care services, and long-term care services. Long-term care organizations often include units engaged in real estate sales and services.

The relevant geographic scopes of labor markets vary directly with the educational qualifications of their participants. The market for unskilled labor is almost certainly local, perhaps confined even to a single district of a large city. The market for pediatric oncologists, however, is national.

Employment mobility can be within cells, as in a career progression within a single organization, or it can cross rows and columns. Labor economists have developed a large body of evidence suggesting that income distributions have just as great a variance within occupations as they do across occupations. The room for career progression within cells is therefore great.

Often, however, cross-cell mobility is important for career development. Large organizations often expect that up-and-coming executives gain experience in a number of occupations (operations, finance, planning, marketing) in a career progression. Organizations that have geographically dispersed operations (including the Veterans Affairs Health System and Tenet Corporation) usually expect geographic variety in their senior managers' backgrounds. Similarly, even within the healthcare sector, movement from one industry (hospital inpatient services, for example) to another (home health) can enhance one's career prospects in an integrated system.

SALARY INCENTIVES

The average compensation levels differ among the cells in the three-dimensional opportunity matrix. On average, for example, senior managers in hospital operations earn higher salaries than can those in long-term care. Those averages, however, mask enormous within-cell differences in compensation. In almost every cell, for example, sharp increases in compensation are associated with seniority. Also in almost every cell, investor-owned organizations pay more, on average, than private not-for-profit organizations, which, in turn, pay more, on average, than government organizations. The size of the differences in compensation among investor-owned, not-for-profit, and government organizations, however, is constrained by market forces. Not-for-profit organizations compete for talent in the same three-dimensional labor markets as do the largest and most successful investor-owned corporations.

EDUCATION AND MOBILITY

Enhancing one's knowledge, skills, and abilities through study and apprenticeship is often an effective way of enhancing career status. Becker (1975) distinguished general training from specific training. General training, like enhancing computer literacy or reading and writing skills, is useful in any occupational setting. Specific training, on the other hand, is useful in only one organization or in only one position. Employers will pay for specific training and will not offer increased compensation for those who complete it. General training, however, enhances one's earning power in many settings, so employers will bid for the services of those who undertake it. Because the individual who takes general training will reap the benefits from it, the individual must bear the cost (often masked by employer-paid educational benefits that are actually traded off for higher wages). General training, in short, enhances opportunities for mobility, within cells and across cells.

NON-MONETARY ISSUES

Not all rewards are monetary. Those who work in healthcare delivery and financing experience the satisfaction of knowing they contribute in very important ways to society's well-being (see the profiles that follow for testimonials). They work in clean environments, and, usually, enjoy the respect of their communities. Such psychic rewards are not unique to any one occupation or industry segment, but are ubiquitous in the opportunity matrix.

Many of the profiles in this book discuss the rewards from performing socially useful work and of providing service to one's community. Others discuss the enjoyment derived from working with interesting, compatible colleagues, and the value of opportunities for upward mobility. Clearly, many of the individuals profiled here could receive greater monetary rewards if they did not value these non-monetary benefits so highly.

SALARY DATA

Given the wide range of positions in which healthcare managers work, it is difficult to gather (and to interpret) information on their earnings. The U.S. Bureau of Labor Statistics has identified "health service managers" as being in an occupation for which demand will grow more rapidly than the average for all occupations until at least 2008. It also predicts that the fastest growth will be in home health agencies, residential care facilities, and in practitioners' offices and clinics (U.S. Bureau of Labor Statistics 2000).

Hewitt Associates, a consulting and management search firm, gathers data on the compensation of healthcare executives, broken down by occupation and by region of the country. These data are reported in *Modern Healthcare* magazine annually (Kirchheimer 2001). Some of the national median compensation (including fringe benefits and bonuses) levels reported for 2001 were:

- Administrator/President $270,000
- Associate Administrator/COO $210,800
- Chief Financial Officer $153,400
- Director of Information Systems $102,600
- Director of Human Resources $99,700

The median is the value that splits the earnings distribution in half, and masks substantial variation within each cell of the opportunity matrix. Earnings in the West were highest, and earnings in the Southeast were lowest among regions. Although individual managers typically experience increasing earnings over their careers, even within an occupation/industry/locality cell, some younger managers will out-earn some older managers (even within a cell) due to their choices of organization, and, sometimes, due to pure luck.

SUMMARY

Health services executives occupy positions defined along three dimensions: occupation, industry, and location. With planning and continuing education, they can move upward within occupation/industry/location cells and enhance their career prospects by moving from cell to cell.

Demand for qualified health services management professionals is high, is expected to grow rapidly in coming years, and (anecdotal evidence suggests) already exceeds supply (Jaklevic 2000). Thus, career prospects for those who select careers in health administration are indeed bright as the twenty-first century dawns.

REFERENCES

Becker, G. 1975. *Human Capital* 2d ed. New York: Columbia University Press for the National Bureau of Economic Research.

Kirchheimer, B. 2001. "Reaping the Rewards." *Modern Healthcare* July 30, 27–33, 38.

Jaklevic, M.C. 2000. "Wanted: A Few Good Leaders." *Modern Healthcare* October 2, 38–40.

Lehr, R.I., McLean, R.A., and Smith, G.L. 1994. "The Legal and Economic Environment." In *Strategic Management of Human Resources in Health Services Organizations*, edited by M.D. Fottler, S.R. Hernandez, and C.L. Joiner, 26–58. Albany, New York: ITP/Delmar.

North American Industrial Classification System Association. [Online source; retrieved 9/28/01]: http://www.naics.com.

United States Bureau of Labor Statistics. 1991. *Dictionary of Occupational Titles*, 4th ed., Vol. 1. Washington, D.C.: U.S. Government Printing Office.

United States Bureau of Labor Statistics. 2000. *Occupational Outlook Handbook, 2000–2001 edition*. Washington, D.C.: U.S. Government Printing Office.

CHAPTER FOUR

Beginning Your Career in Health Services Management

WHERE AND HOW you begin your career will largely depend on what you bring to it and where you want to go. If you do not have a graduate degree in health administration and are already working in healthcare, you should consider returning to school to obtain a master's degree, the terminal professional educational credential for people in this field. A number of options for completing a master's degree exist, including part-time and executive programs that allow for maintaining employment while acquiring an advanced degree.

If you entered graduate school directly from undergraduate studies, you may want to consider completing a postgraduate fellowship. A fellowship is a preceptor-directed program that focuses on nurturing independence and learning through measurement and evaluation of progress toward defined educational objectives. It provides practical learning experience in a healthcare organization beyond graduate-level academic instruction and residency experience, and usually lasts one to two years. A fellowship offers early careerists exposure to senior executives and a broad view of the organization that may not be available in a first job.

Some fellowships are general in nature, while others specialize in healthcare systems, specialty hospitals, academic medical centers, managed care, or group practice management. Though the sponsoring organization may later offer a fellow permanent employment, the organization has no commitment to do so, and a postgraduate fellow has no commitment to accept an offer if one is made. The American College of Healthcare Executives posts information about fellowships and a list of fellowships offered by healthcare organizations on its website (http://www.ache.org).

If you had experience prior to entering a graduate program, you may choose not to pursue a fellowship. You may continue employment in your current organization, either in the same or a different role, or you may seek a job in another healthcare organization where you can more fully use your new knowledge and skills.

TRANSITIONS FOR THE NEW MANAGER

All new managers must make a number of transitions to this role. For those who have gone directly from the world of school to the world of work, moving from school to the responsibilities and challenges of a first full-time professional job will be a major transition. For those who enter health services management from a clinical profession, their new role may be much different from the one they held previously. Moving successfully through all these transitions will provide an essential foundation for the rest of your career.

In a study of new managers, Linda Hill (1992) of the Harvard Business School found that becoming a manager means coming to terms with the difference between the "myth of management and the reality." When people first become managers, they tend to rely heavily on formal authority, that is, getting people to do what they want because they are the "boss." However, as a new manager, you will quickly discover that formal authority is a very limited source of power. Subordinates may not accept you—particularly if you are younger or have less work experience—and peers and bosses do not have to listen to you. Yet all of these groups are critical to your success. As a new manager, you will come to realize the reality of management is more about negotiating and building relationships than exercising formal authority.

If you have come to healthcare management after working as a clinical professional, you will go from being an individual contributor to being a facilitator of others' work and a network builder. You will move from being focused on the relatively independent use of your technical and clinical skills to being someone who is responsible for facilitating the work of others. You will no longer be the direct caregiver but rather someone who has the responsibility to take a broader, more holistic view of the healthcare process. You will be more removed from patients and healthcare outcomes, your relationship to the outcome of care will be more ambiguous, and the instant gratification of helping a patient in need will be absent. The reward of management work is helping others to perform well and seeing them succeed in their work.

BALANCING SKILL SETS

As you move through your career, you must continually and successfully negotiate many transitions. One important series of transitions involves using different skills as your career progresses. Thomas Dolan (1998), the president and chief executive officer of the American College of Healthcare Executives, has said that while certain competencies are needed by all healthcare executives, the level of importance of these skills changes depending on the stage of a person's career. Using the right skills in a balanced way and continuing to learn and acquire new skills are keys to a healthcare professional's career advancement.

Early careerists must have strong technical (e.g., financial, marketing, information systems) skills and will rely on these skills in finding and succeeding in their first jobs. As you progress in your career, additional technical skills will be acquired, but more importantly, you must focus on the development of interpersonal skills. The ability to work collaboratively with others, including other executives, physicians, nurses, and staff, is essential in moving forward in your career.

Technical skills will remain important mid-career and at the senior executive level, and, since healthcare changes quickly, continuous learning, as well as updating and enhancing technical skills, will be necessary. However, at mid-career and senior levels, interpersonal skills become even more important. Mid-career managers must feel comfortable interacting with people at all levels and must be able to communicate effectively with a wide variety of people across the organization. By mid-career, healthcare managers must be able to plan and budget, organize, and staff to accomplish organizational goals and objectives, control organizational processes, and problem solve when there are difficulties with process outcomes (Kotter 1990).

At the senior level, healthcare executives need a broad understanding of the healthcare environment and the organization in which they work. They must be effective communicators both inside and outside the organization. Most of all, senior executives must be leaders. They must be able to set direction and articulate a vision for the organization, align people to understand and achieve the vision, and motivate and inspire people to keep them moving in the right direction despite inevitable obstacles (Kotter 1990).

As may be obvious, the only constant in a health services management career is transition and change, not only in the healthcare environment and in healthcare organizations, but also changes in yourself as a manager or executive. Personal growth and making the necessary transitions throughout your career will require flexibility, personal awareness, and a commitment to lifelong learning.

MENTORING

Healthcare administration, perhaps more than most other management areas, has historically taken very seriously mentoring and the role of more experienced managers and executives in assisting the development of new managers. Many executives are actively engaged in mentoring students, interns, residents, fellows, and early careerists. The American College of Healthcare Executives has issued a professional policy statement on the "Responsibility for Mentoring." This statement recognizes that "healthcare executives have a responsibility to mentor both those entering the field as well as mid-careerists preparing to lead the healthcare system of tomorrow" (ACHE

1999). We encourage early careerists actively to seek out mentors who can help them in their career development but also to consider being mentors themselves.

Finding Mentors

Mentors can assist you as you grow and develop as a manager and executive. Finding people who can be role models, offer constructive advice and feedback, help you evaluate your own strengths and weaknesses, answer questions you have, and promote you to others is an invaluable career asset.

The word "mentor" comes from the character Mentor in Greek mythology; Mentor was Odysseus' trusted counselor. *The American Heritage Dictionary* (2000) defines a mentor as "a wise and trusted counselor or teacher." In today's professional environment, relationships between junior and senior colleagues who contribute to career development are referred to as mentor relationships. Studies have pointed to two broad functions of mentoring for the junior colleague: career functions and psychosocial functions (Kram 1986). While career functions aid the junior colleague's advancement up the hierarchy of an organization, psychosocial functions can contribute to the junior colleague's sense of self-worth and confidence. Career functions of mentoring include:

- *Sponsorship*: Opening doors for the junior colleague through the senior colleague's contacts.
- *Coaching*: Teaching the junior colleague "the ropes" of the organization through feedback on performance, potential, and ways to improve.
- *Protection*: Providing support for the junior colleague, with the senior colleague acting as a buffer when necessary.
- *Exposure*: Creating opportunities for the junior colleague to develop and demonstrate visible competence.
- *Challenging work*: Stretching the junior colleague's knowledge and skills to stimulate growth and prepare him or her for advancement.

Psychosocial functions include:

- *Role modeling*: Demonstrating appropriate values, attitudes, and skills to aid the junior colleague.
- *Counseling*: Providing a helpful and confidential atmosphere for exploring personal and professional dilemmas.
- *Acceptance and confirmation*: Providing on-going support, respect, and admiration, reinforcing the junior colleague's self-confidence and a positive self-image.
- *Friendship*: Mutual caring, intimacy, and interest that extends beyond the immediate work setting.

As an early careerist, you will experience a period of exploration, initiation, and new beginnings. You are acquiring new skills and knowledge, as well as new values, attitudes, and behavior, all of which will contribute to your confidence, competence, and future possibilities for advancement. Mentoring relationships can be extremely valuable during this period, as well as later in your career.

While some of the most important mentoring relationships for early careerists are typically with more senior colleagues, peers and subordinates can provide a number of the mentoring functions outlined above. An example of this would be the relationship of a young manager who has not yet worked in healthcare forming a mentoring relationship with a subordinate who has many years of experience in the healthcare field. Since no one relationship can possibly offer all of the mentoring functions you may want and need, you may find it helpful, if not essential, to have multiple mentors, with each relationship fulfilling a different set of functions for you.

Some organizations have formal mentoring programs that are structured and arranged by the organization (McCauley and Douglas 1998). In these programs, junior colleagues are typically assigned to senior colleagues, inside or outside the direct reporting line in the hierarchy. However, most people will find the search for mentors to be a personal quest. In some cases, a possible mentor may approach you; at other times, you will initiate the relationship. In your quest for mentors, you may want to consider the following questions:

- Is this a person I and others, both inside and outside the organization, respect and admire? Would I want to be like this person? Would I want others to associate me with this person?
- Does this person have the experience, rank, and influence in the organization to provide the career functions I am seeking from a mentor?
- Is this a person I can trust and who trusts me? Is this someone who will be honest with me and with whom I can be honest? Is this a person who has my best interests at heart? Can this person and I be mutually self-disclosing? (These questions will be very important in thinking about the psychosocial functions of the mentoring relationship.)
- Is this a person who can appreciate and be honest about our differences? Can this person see our differences as ways to enhance, rather than limit, the mentoring relationship? (This may be especially important in cross-gender or cross-race mentoring relationships.)
- Does this person have a personal, demonstrated commitment to lifelong learning?
- Is this person willing to take the time and effort to make a personal commitment to my development?

Some mentoring relationships will last throughout your career and develop into deep friendships, while others will be more limited in time and scope. All mentoring relationships require real work and investment from both parties and can produce benefits and personal satisfaction for both.

Being a Mentor

Having mentors can make a huge positive difference in your career, as many of our contributors attest in their profiles. Mentoring relationships can help you better understand yourself as a manager, identify knowledge and skills that you need to develop, and expand opportunities for growth and professional advancement. But even as an early careerist it is important that you help others in their career progression.

By becoming a mentor to others, you will continue to develop your own skills and also help ensure that future administrators are prepared for the challenges they will face. Mentoring can assist you in strengthening your coaching and leadership skills and in learning to work closely with people who are different from you. Through mentoring, you make a contribution to your organization by assisting coworkers and subordinates to grow and develop, thereby retaining talent in the organization. And you can contribute to the field by ensuring that health administration recruits and retains bright, committed people as future leaders.

As an early careerist, here are some ways you can be a mentor:

- Volunteer to represent your organization at high school, college, and university "career fairs." Students may relate especially well to you, since you have recently made some of the same educational and career decisions they are making.
- Work with your undergraduate or graduate program's alumni organization as a mentor to students who are currently preparing for health administration careers. Local ACHE affiliates may also provide similar opportunities to mentor students.
- Communicate with interns, residents, and fellows working in your organization. Offer to be of help to them. Consider asking them to lunch. Tell them about your work and ask them about their career aspirations.
- If you are still a student, volunteer to help with student recruitment and new student orientation. Many graduate programs have "student mentor" activities for second year students to welcome and assist new students.
- Work with peers in mentoring relationships. While many mentoring relationships are between junior and senior colleagues, peer-to-peer relationships can serve important mentoring functions, too.

By being a mentor to a student, intern, resident, fellow, or peer, you can enhance your skills, expand your professional network, and make a contribution to the future of the profession early in your career.

GETTING INVOLVED

Getting involved in professional and community activities can provide incredible growth opportunities for early careerists. Earlier we discussed the importance of a commitment to lifelong learning. Becoming affiliated with a professional association can be an important avenue to lifelong learning, enabling you to gain new skills and keep your knowledge current, as well as expand your network of professional colleagues. These associations typically provide opportunities for continuing education and professional advancement, with the highest level of achievement being "fellowship" in most organizations. You may also choose to take on a service role (e.g., an officer or committee member) in your chosen professional association. This will help you develop your leadership skills and also further the interests of the profession. A number of professional associations for health services executives are listed in the appendix. No doubt you will find one that meets your professional role and aspirations.

Another way to be involved professionally is through the alumni association of your undergraduate or graduate health administration program. Alumni associations provide an outstanding way to stay in touch with your educational "home" and to be in contact with students who will become the future leaders in the field. It may be possible for you to mentor current students in the program through your alumni association connection. Some alumni associations provide continuing education opportunities and some associations provide career counseling and placement services to alumni throughout their careers. Taking a service position in your alumni group can provide excellent opportunities to enhance your leadership skills and enlarge your professional network.

Many health administrators see community service as an obligation that they gladly take on as a way to "give back" to the community. Serving on the board of a local not-for-profit organization can not only provide important development opportunities but can help you make contacts outside your organization and raise the visibility of your organization in the community. Doing hands-on work with organizations like Habitat for Humanity, a shelter for the homeless, or a soup kitchen can provide valuable experience in working with people who are different from you and in developing your ability to work collaboratively with others, outside the usual hierarchy of your organization. It can also reinforce your own sense of service, something that is extremely valuable to leaders at senior levels in healthcare organizations. Many early careerists also find working with organizations like United Way—perhaps as a "loaned" executive—can be very helpful to their development as well.

SUMMARY

Beginning your career in healthcare management is exciting, but for many early careerists it can also be a bit intimidating or overwhelming. How can you make a contribution to the organization where you work, the community where you live, and the profession you have chosen? What is the best path to take to ensure your own success and satisfaction as a healthcare professional? How do you begin, and what steps should you take next? Building relationships with others and focusing on opportunities for growth and development are important ways to find the best answers to these questions.

The profiles that follow in this book will give you insight into how 51 healthcare executives have answered these and other questions about their careers. You will see there are no "right" answers to these questions. We hope you will find this reassuring as you begin your career and see the path ahead of you as a real journey and adventure.

REFERENCES

American College of Healthcare Executives. 1999 (revised). "Responsibility for Mentoring." *Professional Policy Statement*. Chicago: ACHE.

The American Heritage Dictionary of the English Language, 4th ed. 2000. Boston: Houghton Mifflin Co.

Dolan, T.C. 1998. "A Balance of Skills." *Healthcare Executive*, Sept/Oct,: 5.

Hill, L.A. 1992. *Becoming a Manager*. Boston: Harvard Business School Press.

Kotter, J.P. 1990. *A Force for Change: How Leadership Differs from Management*. New York: The Free Press.

Kram, K.E. 1986. "Mentoring in the Workplace." In *Career Development in Organizations*, edited by D.T. Hall and Associates, 160–201. San Francisco: Jossey.

McCauley, C.D., and Douglas, C.A. 1998. "Developmental Relationships." In *Handbook of Leadership Development*, edited by C.D. McCauley, R.S. Moxley, and E. VanVelsor, 160–193. San Francisco: Jossey-Bass.

PART TWO

A Reader's Guide to the Profiles

ASK 1,000 EIGHT-YEAR-OLDS what they want to be when they grow up, and not one of them will say "a healthcare manager." Ask a sample of high school seniors interested in the health professions what courses of study they want to pursue, and one will find prospective physicians, nurses, dentists, and (maybe) physical therapists and pharmacists—but probably not a single health executive. Nonetheless, the occupations that we group together as "health services management" attract new entrants every year, bringing bright young talent to join the ranks of those already in the professions.

The profiles that follow describe, in managers' own words, the career paths of healthcare administrators. We asked each member of our sample to address a few questions:

- How did you become interested in a career in healthcare management?
- How did you prepare yourself?
- What have been your greatest challenges?
- What advice would you give to someone thinking about entering the field?

We have edited the profiles to ensure consistent format, but have attempted not to change their message or meaning in any way.

As you read the profiles, you cannot help being struck by the diversity among the managers. They are diverse in the occupational titles they hold, they are diverse in the industry segments in which they are employed, and they are diverse in the geographical locations in which they live and work. They are, in short, broadly distributed in the three-dimensional opportunity matrix described previously in chapter 3. At the end of this chapter we have included a two-dimensional "Matrix of Profiles" (broken down by occupation and industry segment), based on current employment, as a quick reference to the professionals profiled in the pages that follow.

The contributors to this volume are also diverse in the personal and educational paths they took to their current positions. They demonstrate that no one "right" way to prepare for a career in health administration exists. They studied at distinguished universities, at work-a-day institutions, and in the "school of hard knocks." They hold graduate degrees in health administration, public health, business administration, law, and other fields. A few work in occupations such as law and financial management that require specialized training, but the majority prepared for general management positions. A few have clinical training, but have adopted management as their profession; their clinical degrees have become "deep background" for their work. Some prepared for civilian careers in military service.

The contributors to this volume are also diverse as individuals. We attempted to assemble a broad sample of professionals, and, in that, we have been successful. Women and minorities are, perhaps, overrepresented in these pages. That is by design, as we want to demonstrate the opportunities available in the health services sector. The profiles include some who are at the peaks of distinguished careers, as well as some who are only beginning to distinguish themselves. We have included profiles of several of our academic colleagues, as they represent both the range of opportunities within, and the vitality of, the health administration professorate.

As chapter 3 suggests, many of the individuals profiled here have "jumped around" professionally. The reader will find individuals who have moved, occupationally, from academia to association leadership, from operations to academia, from hospital nursing to operations management, and from dentistry to financial analysis. Our sample also includes individuals who have moved, industrially, from group practice to hospitals, from military medicine to academic medicine, and from free-standing hospitals to integrated systems. Clearly, diversity is possible within a single career, as well as across the sample.

The members of our sample have been, and continue to be, highly mobile. In the short period during which we wrote this book, several of them have moved to new positions.

An interesting aspect of many of the careers described here is the circuitous nature of the routes that lead to health services management. Because very few individuals grow up wanting to be healthcare managers, those who enter these occupations must participate in processes of discovery. Several of the profiles mention influential mentors or role models. Some allude to interesting undergraduate courses and majors. Some were plucked from clinical positions to act as managers. For all of these individuals, healthcare has proven an interesting and rewarding arena, even if not the one they originally intended to pursue.

Many of the individuals here have achieved distinction within one or more of the major professional associations (a list of these appears as an appendix to this volume). One of the major functions of the professional associations (American College of Healthcare Executives, Medical Group Management Association, and others) is the development and sponsorship of continuing education programs. We are unanimous in the belief that lifelong, continuing personal and professional development is a key element of success in any occupation or industry. We encourage the reader to take the examples in our sample seriously.

Another function of the professional associations is to facilitate professional contacts. No professional achieves success in isolation (in fact, the existence of a community is integral to the definition of a profession). Participation in the activities of a relevant professional association is an important way to learn and grow within an occupation or an industry.

Although many of the individuals who contributed to this volume have achieved success without conscious career plans, others have moved deliberately through a series of positions to develop the skills, knowledge, and abilities necessary for senior management. One of the advantages of military career progression is the grooming received in the various medical service corps. That grooming is demonstrated in several of the profiles presented here.

Finally, you will be struck by the joy (no other word is adequate) that the contributors experience in their work and in their careers. Although there may be some self-selection bias in the sample, one cannot help being impressed by the sense of accomplishment and purpose that these men and women experience and that they reflect in their writing. The chance to share that joy is the best reason to discover the opportunities that exist in health administration.

MATRIX OF PROFILES

Occupational Categories					
Industry Segments	Senior Management	Operations Management	Finance	Professional Specialization	Teaching and Academic Administration
Hospital	Howell Hummer Leon Lerner	Bolden Kini Quintana		D'Amico Harlen Valuck	
Integrated System	Allison Eck Omer Pelham Rocklage Taylor	Bonney Dickson Frey Udall	Henley	Vazquez- Morris	
Group Practice		Davenport Williams			
Long-term Care	Rogers				
Insurance and Managed Care		Baroff		Chittalia Stewart	
Consulting				Perry Peterson Vestal Zasa	
Military	VanLandingham		Macus		
Academic					Aaronson Chatman Porter Prybil White
Professional or Trade Association	Clarke Dolan Kahn	Perlman		Mologne Schonfeld	
Related Corporation			Jay	Dwyer Dye Kayser Lenzner Tyler	

William E. Aaronson

Associate Professor of Healthcare Management, Fox School of Business and Management and Associate Director for Health Planning and Policy, Center for Public Health
Temple University
Philadelphia, Pennsylvania

B.S., General Science, Villanova University (Pennsylvania)
M.Ed., Rehabilitation Counseling, Temple University (Pennsylvania)
Ph.D., Business Administration (Organization and Management),
Temple University

I HAVE OFTEN explained my decision to enter health administration as an unintended consequence of my strong clinical skills as a caseworker and team leader. While working as a caseworker, I earned a master's degree in rehabilitation counseling, believing that was where my talents and interests were. At 26 years of age, however, I was asked to manage a 150-bed unit of a long-term care facility, with roughly 160 employees, including physicians, nurses, and support personnel. I had no management education or training to speak of.

There were no part-time master's degree programs in health administration available to me, and I already one master's degree. I found a doctoral program in health administration at Temple University that would allow me to study on a part-time basis, and I spent the next seven years studying and working—essentially two full-time commitments. In the end, I received my doctoral degree, which led to a career change.

Because of my success as a caseworker, and the fact that I was relatively articulate, I was selected to testify in a federal lawsuit lodged against my employer. *Haldeman v. Pennhurst* is a landmark Supreme

Court decision that has helped to define the rights of the institutionalized disabled. My testimony at trial and the succeeding seven years shaped my philosophy and understanding of management and leadership. We lived and worked "in a fishbowl" as we implemented quality improvement programs, developed critical pathways for "habilitation" of the severely disabled, established clinical protocols, and became consumer friendly. By the time I "retired" from active management, state inspectors held us up as a model long-term care facility.

In 1984, I accepted my first faculty appointment in health administration at the Medical University of South Carolina (Charleston). I quickly discovered that in teaching healthcare management courses I could draw on a wealth of personal experience. This put a healthy spin on my lectures and class assignments. Since then, I have held faculty appointments at Widener University in Chester, Pennsylvania, and Temple University in Philadelphia. I have continually tried to remain close to the healthcare industry through consulting and research. At present, I manage a long-term partnership grant between my university, healthcare organizations in Philadelphia, and our counterparts in Kyiv, Ukraine, to develop community-based primary care clinics. This project, along with management training I have provided in former Soviet countries since 1994, is the single most rewarding experience of my career.

The most important advice I can give to someone entering the field is to do whatever job you are doing at present to the best of your ability. Management positions are fewer and farther between than they were previously, so new graduates are likely to enter non-managerial positions (such as business development, program coordination, or financial analysis). A strong work ethic is highly valued; people skills (cross-cultural, team, and interpersonal) are critical. I believe that these attributes were largely responsible for steering my career, as opposed to my career planning, which has been virtually non-existent.

Joel T. Allison

President and Chief Executive Officer
Baylor Health Care System
Dallas, Texas

B.A., Journalism and Religion, Baylor University (Texas)
M.S., Health Care Administration, Trinity University (Texas)
Fellow, American College of Healthcare Executives

I CONSIDER MY work at Baylor Health Care System a "calling." Planning to enter seminary and spend my life in ministry, I took an unprecedented detour, or rather "tour," of a small town Texas hospital that changed my life course. While touring a hospital in Uvalde, Texas, an individual made reference to the fact that they were looking for an administrator and had invited a young man who was going into the ministry to complete his education in hospital administration. The lights flashed "hospital administration and the ministry;" as a result, I combine my passions—ministry and healthcare.

I received a bachelor's degree in journalism and religion at Baylor University in 1970 and attended Trinity University's healthcare administration program, where I earned a master's degree in 1973. Upon completion of the administrative residency program at Hendrick Medical Center in Abilene, I served on the administrative staff there for ten years.

Before joining Baylor Health Care System in 1993 as chief operating officer, I was president and chief executive officer of Driscoll Children's Hospital in Corpus Christi from 1987 to 1993. Prior to that, I was chief executive officer of Northwest Texas Hospital in Amarillo and president of Methodist Medical Center in St. Joseph, Missouri.

Currently, I serve as president and chief executive officer of Baylor Health Care System (BHCS) in Dallas. My primary responsibility is to help Baylor attain its vision of becoming the world's "most trusted source of comprehensive health services." I maintain a focus on providing high quality, safe patient care that can be measured and reported. I also place a renewed focus on medical education and healthcare research and continue to collaborate with physicians in the design and development of BHCS. Patients are our priority. When we provide the best care available, then we've done our job. Determining how to serve and preserve what Baylor has and stands for and how to continue to respect and honor the past while creating the future is my challenge.

I am a Fellow of the American College of Healthcare Executives. In addition, I serve as chairman of the board of directors of the Health Careers Foundation, a national organization that raises funds for students pursuing careers in allied health fields, and as chairman of Novation, a national healthcare supply chain management organization that is affiliated with the Voluntary Hospitals of American.

With the many demands on my time, I believe in bringing a balance to life—in your spiritual life, family life, and professional life. God is first, family is second, and the job is third. If any one of the three gets out of balance, the other two are affected. Being healthy in mind, body, and spirit is important for a balanced life as well.

Marina Baroff

Assistant Area Administrator
Kaiser Permanente Medical Care Program
San Diego, California

B.A., Psychology, University of North Carolina–Chapel Hill
M.A., Counseling, George Washington University (Washington, D.C.)
M.P.H., University of California–Berkeley
Fellow, American College of Healthcare Executives

FOR THE PAST 13 years I have been an assistant area administrator for the San Diego, California, area of Kaiser Permanente Medical Care Program, which services 500,000 members. In this role, I have directed business services, quality/utilization, clinical, surgical, and operations support, and information management departments for a 376-bed hospital and 27 medical and office buildings. In addition to my administrative responsibilities, I have also led activities in breast cancer screening, e-commerce, Y2K, capital project, physician-patient relations, service guarantee, patient-focused care, quality assurance integration, and threat management.

I am a Fellow in the American College of Healthcare Executives and serve on the Board of Governors as Governor for District 7. I have previously served as a board member of the Healthcare Executives Association of San Diego/Imperial Counties and president of San Diego Women in Health Administration.

Prior to joining Kaiser Permanente, I worked as a planner for a county health department, an administrator of a hospital-based clinic, a senior analyst for a university health affairs office, and an administrator of HMO outpatient health centers, all in the San Francisco Bay Area.

My educational background includes a master's degree in public health from the University of California–Berkeley and a master's degree in counseling psychology from the George Washington University. I've lived in California for 22 years, but grew up in North Carolina. I don't have much of a Southern accent though, because I was born and spent my "wonder bread years" in New York City.

My interest in healthcare grew out of an involvement in the women's movement during college and dashed my hopes to be an international spy. As a young adult, I demonstrated for the passage of the Equal Rights Amendment, took a number of women's studies courses, and became a volunteer at a local rape crisis center. Although I was officially a psychology major, I also had a concentration in Russian studies with coursework in language, history, political science, and literature. Unfortunately, with the Cold War still in full swing, the only job prospects open to Russian studies majors were within the intelligence community. While I had read a great many spy novels and fantasized about life undercover, my pragmatic side took over, and I went to graduate school in counseling psychology.

While in graduate school, I had a series of part-time jobs in women's health both at a local level in a clinic setting and for a national women's health organization. The more exposure I had to healthcare, the more interested I became in obtaining a recognized health credential. So after finishing my first advanced degree, I decided to pursue a degree in public health. This coursework officially launched my career in healthcare management.

Once I completed public health training, I focused my energies on working for a local government doing program planning and evaluation. Later, as I gained management experience in clinics, hospitals, and health plans in Northern and Southern California, I developed a great appreciation for both the challenges and rewards of my chosen profession and also crafted my own personal mission and vision. This mission is to improve the health of the community and encourage greater collaboration between public health and medical care. From a job perspective, my vision is to serve in a key executive role in an organization that embraces a holistic view of health. Such an organization will recognize that lifestyle, environment, and genetics largely determine health status. It will also understand that although medical care is a factor in the health equation, it has a relatively minor role.

I believe that the most difficult obstacles to overcome in healthcare administration are to shift resources from treatment to prevention and to pioneer change without a strong base of physician support. Both of these elements are critical to the success of improved health outcomes for the general population.

Throughout my career, the most rewarding experiences have been to mentor, coach, and provide leadership lessons to my direct-report managers, and to serve in leadership roles for a local women's health-care executive group and for the American College of Healthcare Executives. My advice to early careerists is to make a commitment to life-long learning, seek to balance program or operations experience with macro/policy work, do your homework, tactfully question authority, always follow through on commitments, and have fun.

James L. Bolden

Health Services Project Administrator
Balm of Gilead Center
Cooper Green Hospital
Birmingham, Alabama

B.S., Medical Technology, University of Alabama at Birmingham
M.P.A., University of Alabama at Birmingham

 I ENTERED THE field of health administration to have an impact on the delivery of healthcare services in the community. I felt that healthcare management best matched my skills and interests and would afford an opportunity to serve in a leadership role in helping to provide healthcare services to those in need.

I entered healthcare management directly out of college in 1987, as a laboratory supervisor with the Alabama region of the American Red Cross. The experience was great. It gave me the opportunity to really develop my people skills. After two years, I had the opportunity to advance to the position of assistant technical director. After two months our technical director was also promoted, and I then served as interim technical director for the remainder of that year. I continued to serve as assistant director for an additional two years

In 1990, the American Red Cross consolidated donor testing around the country. For the Alabama region it meant shifting the testing of donors to a facility an Atlanta. This resulted in the closing of the testing laboratory in Birmingham and a significant downsizing in technical services. My position was phased out; however I was given the opportunity to work in a similar capacity in Georgia. I opted to remain in

Birmingham and accept a medical technologist position with the University of Alabama at Birmingham (UAB) Hospital in its blood bank.

The experience with the blood bank gave me the opportunity to have direct patient contact and provide hands-on care for people with various medical conditions. During this time I also entered the master of public administration (MPA) program at UAB. I felt that a MPA combined with my healthcare management experience from the Red Cross and my direct patient care experience with UAB would give me greater insight into any future administrative duties.

After I completed graduate school in 1997, I found that my previous experience, while rich in healthcare functions, gave some potential employers the impression that I was too technical for other administrative positions. I then began to work with the strategic planning committee for hospital laboratories at UAB Hospital and volunteered with various policy and procedure development projects.

In early 1998, I applied for and started working in administration at UAB as a strategic planning analyst. In this role, I was responsible for providing research and analytical assistance in describing strategic conditions and making recommendations to management for specific planning strategies and tactics.

While working as an analyst, I became aware of a new startup program in town. The program—the Balm of Gilead Project—was a palliative care program based at Cooper Green Hospital, the public hospital for Jefferson County. I applied for and was accepted for the position of project administrator, responsible for the development and oversight of program operations, including strategic planning, grant compliance, and fundraising activities. Because the Balm of Gilead's patients are the poor, the uninsured, and the homeless, this is a very challenging, but rewarding, position.

My advice to anyone entering the field is to be aware of the environment you're working in and be prepared to take advantage of new opportunities.

Robert S. Bonney

Vice President-Managed Care
St. Luke's Shawnee Mission Health System
Kansas City, Missouri

A.B., Mathematics, College of the Holy Cross (Massachusetts)
M.B.A., Finance and Personnel Management, University of Missouri–Columbia
M.S.P.H., Health Services Management, University of Missouri–Columbia
J.D., Detroit College of Law
Fellow, American College of Healthcare Executives

 AFTER RECEIVING MY MBA, I pursued an MSPH in health services management, believing that health administration, with the recent enactment of Title 18, was a field that could utilize my skills. As part of this program, I was fortunate to do a summer internship with a dynamic administrative staff at a large public teaching hospital with a highly action-oriented CEO. Following graduation, I accepted a position on this hospital's staff and was given immediate management responsibilities, including the area of patient accounts. This early position offered me a chance to learn about the operations of a hospital.

While in my first position, I had the opportunity to pursue a law degree in the evenings. These studies helped strengthen my analytical skills and have proven to be an invaluable adjunct to my training.

I then moved to another large teaching hospital. This position turned out not to be a good fit with the management style I had developed, and I left after only two and one-half years. I moved to an emerging integrated delivery system, where I stayed for thirteen years. I was involved in all aspects of the system's development and with many unique projects. My last position with this system was serving simultaneously as the chief operating officer for the system's two largest hospitals while maintaining several staff and line responsibilities.

I then moved to the executive director role in a 170,000-member managed care organization. This experience gave me firsthand working knowledge of a managed care organization and prepared me for my current role as vice president of managed care for the Saint Luke's Shawnee Mission Health System in Kansas City, Missouri. I also now serve as senior vice president for product line management and have once again assumed line management responsibilities.

As I review my career, a major factor to success has been a willingness to seek out and assume whatever responsibilities the organization might offer. Diversity of experience is the key to growth and development of one's career. Throughout my career I have been involved in teaching graduate students and executives in healthcare management. I have also had the opportunity to author or coauthor numerous articles, book chapters, and two books. Being able to give back to the field is important to me, since it has provided me with a rich and fulfilling career.

The greatest challenge I have faced has been in balancing the need to run the business of healthcare with the imperative to maintain a high standard of quality. The most rewarding experiences I have had include implementing a new program for the community, working with a team on a complicated project that took three years to complete, facilitating the integration of the management of several hospitals, helping develop future healthcare leaders, and being able to teach both practicing executives and traditional master's students.

The advice I would give to someone entering the field is to remember that the decisions you make will shape the healthcare delivery system of the future—a system that one day you will need. Do not forget the patient, since you will likely be one someday.

Vera Stevens Chatman

Professor of the Practice and Director of Health and Human Services
Department of Human and Organizational Development
Vanderbilt University
Nashville, Tennessee

B.A., Psychology, Fisk University (Tennessee)
M.A., Psychology, Fisk University
Ph.D., School of Psychology, Vanderbilt University (Tennessee)

 I CHOSE A career in health services administration following the counsel of several supportive mentors who helped me realize that this field would give me the opportunity to fulfill my passions of nurturing others and helping to open nontraditional professions to minorities.

In 1975, shortly before the completion of my doctorate, I accepted my first professional job at Meharry Medical College, a historically black medical center complex. I remained there for 20 years, during which time I held a variety of positions including coordinator of research and evaluation and director of the Elam Mental Health Center, administrative director for the clinical research center, and director of the division of community health science, which awards a master of science degree in public health. During my tenure as director of the division, I worked to obtain its initial accreditation and served as a fellow of the Accrediting Commission on Education for Health Services Administration (ACEHSA). While at Meharry, I also developed the Center on Aging.

In 1995, I came to Vanderbilt University because it provided an opportunity for me to focus on research related to diversity issues in healthcare, organize new health-related programs, and train students in an area that had a shortage of well-qualified professionals. As director of the health and human services program, I am responsible for coordinating the education of undergraduates interested in careers in the helping professions. During the past four years, I have focused on career development over the life span. I also work with the Vanderbilt University Medical Center by serving as director of the statewide Tennessee Governor's School for Health Sciences and serve as the faculty liaison for the BS/MSN in the School of Nursing.

For the past 20 years, I have served as a consultant for and a board member of a number of local, regional, and national professional healthcare organizations. I have also served as a member of national committees to develop policy for several agencies within the U.S. Department of Health and Human Services.

The most consistent theme of my career has been diversity. I have promoted diversity throughout Vanderbilt's college and university systems as well as on the local, state, and national levels. Some of my active involvement includes chairing the Peabody annual reception for graduate and professional students of color, coordinating an assessment of diversity within the Vanderbilt University Medical Center, serving as faculty co-chair for Vanderbilt's annual Martin Luther King Lecture Series, co-chairing the annual Tennessee Minority Health Youth Summit, chairing the Diversity Task Force of the Association of University Programs in Health Administration (AUPHA), and serving as the first chairperson of AUPHA's Diversity Faculty Forum.

One of my greatest challenges occurred early in my career at Meharry Medical College when I was expected to create and maintain quality programs with extremely limited resources. More recently, my greatest challenge has been the transition in roles from administrator to academic teacher and researcher at Vanderbilt. In the administrative role, I was rewarded for quick and often independent decisions that had immediate outcomes. In contrast, academic teaching and research requires a slower-paced, consensus-building approach with input from a number of constituents and frequently delayed results. Another challenge has been the constant struggle to maintain a balance between my career and my family. As a wife and mother of two girls, each day requires a reevaluation of priorities. Personal flexibility, in addition to family and professional support, has made it easier for me to have both a gratifying family life and a rewarding career.

The greatest rewards of my career have been in seeing people benefit from the work I do and from mentoring—from working with high-risk students struggling to achieve even the lowest of expectations or the most ambitious students with the greatest of expectations, to young professionals starting their careers and seasoned professionals nervously seeking career changes.

I have several pieces of advice for anyone entering this field. Always take every assignment as an opportunity to share and to learn. Be creative and flexible in your thinking. Always look for a more effective way to do your job. Don't be eager to be an expert at everything, but strive to be a valuable part of an efficient team.

Ali Z. Chittalia

Senior Analyst
Blue Cross of Northeastern Pennsylvania
Wilkes-Barre, Pennsylvania

M.D., Dr. P.D.M. Medical College of India, Amaravati
M.H.A., University of Scranton (Pennsylvania)

AS A MEDICAL student in India, I was always fascinated by the dynamics of corporate healthcare. When I
graduated from medical school, I wanted to use my
medical expertise to develop efficient health systems for
providing quality care to consumers. From 1993 to
1995, I worked in East Africa and the Middle East as a
clinician, but spent much of my time in the "operations" of clinics,
labs, and hospitals. Having had a taste of management, I decided to
pursue professional training in health administration to sharpen my
business skills. I enrolled in the master of health administration program at the University of Scranton in 1996.

My administrative residency was in a multi-specialty group practice where I developed a physician compensation/incentive model
based on quality, compliance, and production. My elective internship
was in a post–acute delivery center and revolved around implementing a new decision support system. In today's healthcare environment, a trusted management information system is a necessity.

Currently, I work at Blue Cross of Northeastern Pennsylvania as a
senior analyst in contracting and reimbursement. My duties entail
negotiating contracts with hospitals, physicians, and ancillary providers.

I am also responsible for developing fair and equitable reimbursement models for providers that ensure high-quality services for our members. Along with senior management staff, I monitor the HMO performance in terms of utilization of services and propose strategies for improved performance.

My greatest challenge is to control rising healthcare costs in an environment of high expectations from members and providers. Technological advances, better access to services, and a wide variance in provider practice matters contribute to the upward trend in healthcare costs, creating immense challenges. The greatest reward is to ensure high member and provider satisfaction, coupled with the accomplishment of corporate goals and objectives.

With all its complexities and challenges, the healthcare management field makes boredom almost impossible. The industry is moving at a rapid pace, new models of health delivery are emerging, and, hence, there is always something new to learn. Healthcare executives have to be open-minded and flexible, and possess skills in financial management and information systems. For new entrants to the field, I recommend some kind of "payer" experience that will pay off when one moves to the provider side of healthcare delivery, especially in a managed care environment. Stay current in your readings of health management journals and make a commitment to lifelong continuing education. Finally, do not hesitate to ask questions until you have a complete understanding on any academic or professional assignment.

In the future, I would like to pursue doctoral study in health services and to direct projects undertaken by the World Health Organization.

Note: Since this profile was written, Ali Chittalia has become the executive director of the "Healthy Northeast Pennsylvania Initiative," a community project focusing on preventive healthcare.

Richard L. Clarke

President and Chief Executive Officer
Healthcare Financial Management Association
Westchester, Illinois

B.S., Industrial Distribution, Bradley University (Illinois)
M.B.A., University of Miami
Fellow, Healthcare Financial Management Association

 I AM PRESIDENT and chief executive officer of the Healthcare Financial Management Association (HFMA), a professional association with more than 32,000 members in 70 chapters. I have held this position since June of 1986.

Like many of my healthcare financial colleagues, I did not receive formal undergraduate or graduate training in health administration. Rather, I was trained in general business disciplines and hired into an entry-level management position (assistant finance director) at a large public hospital (Jackson Memorial Hospital in Miami). I earned a bachelor of science in industrial distribution (combining business administration and engineering) from Bradley University in Peoria, Illinois, and an MBA (management/finance) from the University of Miami.

From 1980 to 1986, I held positions with Swedish Health Systems of Englewood, Colorado, including chief financial officer and treasurer. During that period, I attained Fellowship in HFMA (1983). I also was president of the Colorado Chapter of HFMA, served on the HFMA National Matrix, and was a member of HFMA's Principles and Practices Board.

I currently write a monthly column for HFMA's magazine, *Health-care Financial Management*. I also have written numerous articles on healthcare finance and have coauthored three books: *The Crisis in Health Care: Costs, Choices and Strategies* (Jossey-Bass 1990); *Capitalizing Medical Groups: Positioning Physicians for the Future* (HFMA and McGraw-Hill 1998); and *Beyond Managed Care: Forces Behind the Growing Role of Consumers and Technology* (Jossey-Bass 2000).

I serve as chair of the board for both AHA Financial Solutions, Inc., a wholly owned for-profit subsidiary of the American Hospital Association, and the corporate sponsors for the Accrediting Commission on Education for Health Services Administration (ACEHSA).

Through on-the-job experience and professional development programs offered by HFMA and others I learned the unique aspects of healthcare finance. These learning opportunities gave me appreciation for the unique aspects of health administration. In retrospect, graduate training in health administration would have helped my grounding in the field and early career advancement.

My advice to those entering the field is this: Take and always hold onto the "system view" of the enterprise. Too often, new graduates are hired into specific areas of the organization (operations, finance, marketing, planning), and view the organization from only those perspectives. To add true value, learn about the entire organization—the business the organization is in and the interrelationship of the parts. Always consider the system of service the organization provides, not just the unique area in which you work. In my experience, those who provide a system view are more frequently asked to serve on important multi-departmental teams and are more likely to be considered for new opportunities.

Sheryle A. D'Amico

Director of Rehabilitation Services
Lawrence Memorial Hospital
Lawrence, Kansas

B.S., Physical Therapy, Simmons College (Massachusetts)
M.H.S.A., University of Kansas

 MY JOURNEY TO the directorship of rehabilitation services could only have been made possible through the master of health services administration program at the University of Kansas. However, the beginning of clinical interest, and my transition to clinical management, began years ago, as a twelve-year-old watching a physical therapist nurture my grandmother back to health from the effects of a devastating stroke. From that time on, I strove to become a physical therapist, graduating in 1983 from Simmons College in Boston. My first position was with Liberty Mutual Medical Service Center, where the clinical focus at was on rehabilitation of the injured worker. Three years later, I moved to Beth Israel Hospital, where I participated in the care of severely injured patients and burn victims and in research with clinical staff from Harvard University.

It was at Beth Israel that I began the transition from a purely clinical therapist to a manager in the clinical environment. My rise to senior therapist was based on demonstrated clinical skill, not on any administrative skill. It is one of the common paradoxes in healthcare that advancement of clinical personnel to administrative positions is based on success as clinicians, rather than on administrative skills.

Movement to an administrative role should require training in budgeting, human resources, and other management fields.

After moving to Kansas, I entered the health services administration graduate program at the University of Kansas, while continuing to work as the outpatient rehabilitation supervisor at St. Francis Hospital and Medical Center in Topeka. During four years of working full-time in Topeka, I completed the 58 credit hours required for the MHSA degree. Though demanding, this degree allowed me to advance to the director level, with the promise of further advancement. The MHSA program has also opened doors in other areas, such as allowing me to become a member of a burn team in a U.S. State Department-funded program, helping to advance burn care throughout the Republic of Kyrgyzstan in Central Asia. I have also been involved in hospital-wide committee work, such as service on the bioethics committee and the clinical quality improvement committee.

Managing healthcare services in this day and age is not without challenges. I believe the greatest challenge we face today is providing excellent clinical care while remaining fiscally responsible. Some believe the two cannot be achieved simultaneously, but I disagree. A value-based leader can lead his or her team to be successful in all aspects of healthcare.

Dale W. Davenport

Administrator
Department of Medicine
Creighton University School of Medicine
Omaha, Nebraska

B.S., Business Administration, Troy State University at Montgomery (Alabama)
M.H.S.A., George Washington University (Washington, D.C.)
Diplomate, American College of Healthcare Executives

ACADEMIC MEDICINE ADMINISTRATION, managing medical schools and their affiliated hospitals, is a recently developed career path within the field of health services administration. Academic medicine is a major part of our health services system, accounting for expenditures of $57 billion annually. Academic medicine has three traditional missions: education, research, and clinical care; but, until recently, most health services management positions were limited to supporting the clinical mission. Management opportunities have increased dramatically in the last decade, however, due to major organizational changes that have occurred in our healthcare system, primarily in managed care and in increased research activity. Medical schools and their teaching hospitals have been transformed into vertically and horizontally integrated healthcare delivery systems, and university research activities have also been reorganized into major business activities.

My career in academic medicine began by accident almost eight years ago. I had viewed my first position in this area as transitional. Having spent 20 years in hospital administration in the U.S. Air Force, I thought this new position would offer a great opportunity to learn more about physician practice management and would lead me back into hospital administration. Hospitals had begun employing physicians and needed managers who could operate large physician groups. I felt my newly acquired knowledge of managing the "physician side" of healthcare would complement my inpatient hospital management skills. I quickly learned that academic medicine is much more than just the physician side of the business and I realized that I had found a new career.

In my current position, I manage the largest department in the university, employing 70 physicians, 15 Ph.D. scientists, and approximately 325 support personnel, with an annual operating budget of $45 million. Our department has 14 divisions organized by medical specialty with responsibilities to support our missions of teaching, research, and patient care. We conduct physician training programs for 60 internal medicine residents and offer advance fellowships in allergy/immunology, pulmonary/critical care, and cardiology.

Our physicians have practice locations throughout the metropolitan area and conduct outreach clinics at about 30 sites in a three-state area. The department operates a fleet of vehicles to transport patients, physicians, technicians, and equipment among our various sites. We also operate a number of clinical and research facilities with high-tech diagnostic and therapeutic equipment including the latest in computer technology.

My greatest challenges have been to eliminate a significant financial deficit, improve productivity, and increase faculty and staff compensation. With great assistance from our department chair, we reorganized our departmental management structure, created a faculty incentive compensation system, and realigned financial accountability. We eliminated our deficit within one year of making the changes. Our faculty members now benefit financially from increases in their productivity and reductions in staffing and other operating expenses. Our support staff is paid at or above market rates, improving recruitment and retention. Our divisions are now responsible for the financial management of their areas and determine their own staffing levels and support service requirements. These changes have created a new group of "owners" who look for opportunities to continue their success.

My academic preparation and health administration experience have been critical factors in achieving success in academic medicine. My organizational and interpersonal skills are challenged on a daily basis in meeting the diverse needs of a highly intelligent faculty and staff. In addition to my full-time duties, I am a past-president of a local affiliate group of the American College of Healthcare Executives and am chair-elect of the Indian Chicano Health Center, a community health center. I also serve on the board of directors of a community consortium of cancer centers involved in clinical research. Recently, I also thoroughly enjoyed teaching a course in the university's MHSA program.

My advice to individuals considering a management career in academic medicine is to become involved in as many professional activities as possible that will enhance your management skills. Your extra efforts will open new doors of opportunity.

Conan Dickson

Assistant Administrator
The Johns Hopkins Outpatient Center
Baltimore, Maryland

B.B.A., Accounting, Auburn University (Alabama)
B.S., Health Systems Management, Auburn University
M.P.H., Health Policy and Administration, Yale University (Connecticut)
Doctoral Candidate, Health Policy and Management, The Johns Hopkins
University (Maryland)

 WITH AN INTEREST in medical school, I spent the summer after my sophomore year working in an emergency department as a volunteer. I discovered the emergency department is an amazing place where everyone there works together for one purpose—to help sick people.

I wanted to be part of such a team, but had difficulty deciding which healthcare job interested me the most. Fortunately, I realized that one position would allow me to take advantage of my inability to decide on a vocation: healthcare administrator. The administrator works with every position in a healthcare setting and serves as a leader, mediator, coordinator, and facilitator to ensure that all the members of a healthcare team work together.

I called a couple of administrators and asked them if I could come and talk with them. They encouraged me to find a major that would allow me to develop skills needed not only to be a leader, but also to run a business. Following their advice, I declared majors in health systems management and accounting. The health administration program required an internship, which taught me the importance of having a mentor, developing relationships with other administrators through a professional society, developing my own management style, and continuing with a graduate level education.

I decided to seek a master of public health (MPH) degree for a variety of reasons. My undergraduate course work already covered many of the basic skills such as finance, management, and marketing, and I was interested in other disciplines such as health policy and epidemiology, which are incorporated into an MPH degree. I also selected a program affiliated with a medical school because I wanted more exposure to clinicians. I even lived in a medical school dorm, which gave me an appreciation for what medical students go through to become a physician.

The hardest lesson for me to learn has been self-confidence. Going from an undergraduate program at a public school in the South to a prestigious Ivy League graduate school in the Northeast was very intimidating for me. Even after I learned that I could be a successful student in this environment, the career services office had to convince me to apply for the administrative fellowship program at The Johns Hopkins Health System. However, I found that I was able to do well, and after my fellowship, I was asked to fill a position as an assistant administrator for outpatient services.

My job is unusual because it is at a huge outpatient facility, a joint venture between The Johns Hopkins School of Medicine and The Johns Hopkins Hospital in inner-city Baltimore. The Johns Hopkins Outpatient Center is a 450,000 square foot facility that has approximately 1,500 patient encounters in nearly 100 subspecialty clinics on a given day. The office of ambulatory operations and practice management is responsible for all administrative, building, and clinical services.

Working here is both challenging and rewarding. The size of the organization makes it challenging to see the "big picture" when trying to deal with daily operations. Imagine the complexities of managing registration when hundreds of different combinations of insurance plans are presented each day. A joint venture means multiple bosses. This has forced me to look at every issue from the perspectives of both the physician practice manager and the hospital administrator. Academic medicine involves the continuous challenge to balance patient care, teaching, and research. As a manager of clinical operations, it is easy to lose sight of the importance of teaching and research. However, teaching and research are what attract incredible physicians.

If you are considering a career in healthcare administration, you will find tremendous challenges. You will also find that healthcare affects every individual's quality of life; you can make a difference in how those services are delivered. A few important lessons can help you on your journey.

- *Find a compatible mission.* Find an organization that is committed to a mission that you believe is important and interesting. Don't limit your search to hospitals; health services are delivered by many organizations that need talented administrators.
- *Education.* Get the right education for your career objective. Specialize in something that will get you an entry-level job; most administrators have to work their way into a management position. Acquire strong computer skills. Knowing how to use database and spreadsheet software is an important advantage.
- *Get your foot in the door.* This is the most intimidating part of the field; however, it is not as difficult as it might seem. The key is to establish relationships. Join the professional organization for what you want to do. Make an appointment with someone who does what you want to do. Do volunteer work or an internship without expecting to get paid.
- *Be productive.* Once you are in a position, be proactive and productive. When I give a project to my staff, I usually tell them everything I know about the project in five minutes and then send them out to see what they can find out. It is always impressive when someone comes back with an attempt rather than giving up because I didn't give precise instructions. I would not send them out to work on the project if I already knew the answer. Also, don't be afraid to submit a draft to your boss. A draft allows for feedback and shows that you are being productive.

Thomas C. Dolan

President and Chief Executive Officer
American College of Healthcare Executives
Chicago, Illinois

B.B.A., Management, Loyola University of Chicago
Ph.D., Hospital and Health Administration, University of Iowa
Fellow, American College of Healthcare Executives

WHEN I BEGAN to consider a career path, I knew that I wanted a profession that would allow me to use my business and organizational skills and to make a positive impact on society. I found that healthcare management provided me that opportunity. To prepare for my career in this field, I earned a bachelor's degree in management from Loyola University in Chicago, as well as a Ph.D. in hospital and health administration from the University of Iowa.

I began my career as an instructor in Iowa's hospital and health administration program and went on to become a visiting fellow at the University of Washington. I then moved on to the University of Missouri—Columbia's School of Health-Related Professions, where I began as an assistant professor and later took on the position of director of graduate studies in health services management. After that, I served as an associate professor and the director of the center for health services education and research at St. Louis University.

I began my career at the American College of Healthcare Executives as a vice president. I then served as executive vice president for four years before becoming president and chief executive officer. In this position, I am responsible for representing the organization to the external environment and ensuring effective working relationships among ACHE 's various divisions. I report directly to a 15-person Board of Governors, supervise 102 full-time staff, and oversee an annual budget of approximately $16 million.

The greatest challenge facing healthcare executives today is providing high-quality care to all people at an affordable cost. Most of my career has revolved around helping other healthcare executives accomplish this. As an academic, I prepared future healthcare executives for the field. At ACHE, I have assisted working professionals in maintaining and enhancing their skills. One of the greatest challenges I face in this era in which everyone already has too much to do and too little time to do it, is promoting the idea that lifelong learning is the key to success. Healthcare executives must make time for continuing education if they are to overcome the challenges of the healthcare marketplace. My greatest reward has been watching individuals with whom I have worked flourish in their careers as they contribute to that goal of providing high-quality care.

The best advice I can offer a person entering this field is to always put your customers and coworkers first. While the healthcare management field will continue to evolve, one thing that will never change is the need for high-quality service to your internal and external customers.

William M. Dwyer

Divisional Vice President
Strategic Marketing
Abbott HealthSystems Division

B.A., Adolescent Psychology, University of Minnesota
M.B.A., J.L. Kellogg Graduate School of Management, Northwestern
University (Illinois)

I JOINED ABBOTT Laboratories in 1977, and spent my early days with the company on the road, working as a salesman. Five years later, I found myself in an office at the company's corporate headquarters near Chicago. Above my desk I noticed a sign that read "Marketing Research." It was the first time I had considered such a concept. Then, not long after I began to interact with my coworkers— most of whom were highly skilled and trained in marketing—I became acutely aware that my degree in adolescent psychology had not adequately provided me with the language, nor the tools, required to excel in the modern business world. At that point I enrolled at Northwestern University's J.L. Kellogg Graduate School of Management and began pursuing a triple major in management, marketing, and health services management (HSM).

Kellogg's HSM program appealed to me for several reasons. First, I believed that health executives would increasingly become involved in the major purchasing decisions that affected Abbott's products, the lifeblood of our company. This theory has been proven true by the successful growth of national group purchasing organizations like VHA/Novation, Premier, and AmeriNet. The second reason behind my decision to enroll at Kellogg was my intense curiosity about leadership in the field of healthcare delivery. I had often wondered what skills were required to lead modern, world-class organizations like Baptist Memorial, Henry Ford, or Northwestern Memorial Health Systems. Finally, having worked as a psychiatric technician during college, I had personally observed how cooperation between administrators, physicians, nurses, and other healthcare professionals played a vital role in achieving excellent patient care outcomes. I thought then, as I do now, that executive leadership is the primary factor in determining just how good the American healthcare delivery system will ever be.

Educators at Kellogg during the mid-80s had a profound impact on my views of the national healthcare landscape. Steve Shortell, Ed Hughes, and Joel Shalowitz had incredible insights into the chaotic world of healthcare delivery, reimbursement trends, and Medicare/Medicaid reforms. I found myself gravitating toward their courses, many of which focused on strategy, research, and leadership. What I learned along the way has served me well throughout my career, and continues to do so in my present position as divisional vice president of strategic marketing.

Just as the term "marketing research" was once foreign to me, the idea of "strategic marketing" was just as foreign to Abbott's Health-Systems Division. It was during my efforts to develop a job description for my current position, which incorporates myriad activities, that I introduced the concept of strategic marketing. Among other responsibilities, I've become an internal futurist/industry observer for the company. Each year, I use what I've learned to compile two executive trend reports known as "Strategic Grand Rounds®" and "Technology Futures Report™."

The art of mentoring was taught at Kellogg and is continuously demonstrated by the people profiled in this book. It also is modeled by Abbott executives, whose mentoring efforts have been vital to my career success. I fully embrace formal mentoring programs and participate as a mentor both at Abbott and for Kellogg's HSM program.

For individuals who thrive on converting challenges to opportunities, now is a great time to enter the field of health services administration. Many experts believe that in the next two decades we will see the most dramatic changes in healthcare coverage since workplace insurance was introduced 50 years ago. The next generation of leaders will be called upon to formulate solutions for issues as important as how to provide insurance to the more than 45 million Americans who are currently uninsured. Personal characteristics like leadership, adaptability, intellect, personal integrity, and vision will be required in future healthcare administrators. Professional degrees like the MHA, MPH, and MBA will remain relevant to the field as formal training will better prepare individuals for early pitfalls that might otherwise trip up a budding career. Nonetheless, the chief executive officer positions at our nation's most prestigious institutions will attract other qualified-by-experience candidates, who will present themselves with advanced degrees from the fields of law, business, medicine, and nursing. While competition is expected, the most direct course will continue to include a degree from a recognized health services administration program.

My path has been unusual, as I have sought the best of two worlds. As a member today of the board of directors of the Banner Health System, I appreciate the lessons I've learned both academically at Kellogg and professionally at Abbott. Leadership is an art that requires careful nurturing and a booster shot of reality-based learning. The industry faces challenges, and its future prospects will be contingent upon how well we prepare the next class of healthcare executives.

Carson F. Dye

Partner and Vice President
Witt Kieffer, Ford, Hadelman & Lloyd
Toledo, Ohio

B.A., Business and Psychology, Marietta College (Ohio)
M.B.A., Xavier University (Ohio)
Fellow, American College of Healthcare Executives

AFTER ALMOST 30 years in the field, 20 as an executive practitioner and almost 10 as a search and management consultant, I continue to approach each day with great excitement. I can think of no other field that provides as much variety, challenge, and range of interactions. The field contains some of the most intelligent people in society, as well as the ability to touch lives at all levels. For many communities, the local hospital is the largest and most prominent institution. It is the prime employer and the locus of societal pride.

My entry into healthcare was not clearly planned. Instead, after an undergraduate program of business/psychology, I looked for an opportunity to apply this combination and found healthcare human resources to provide that avenue. My first job immediately following graduation was spent in a small 60-bed hospital, setting up their first human resources department. This experience provided a base on which I built my career. In total, I worked in four hospitals in human resources executive positions for twenty years, including the small hospital experience as well as serving as the chief human resources executive in a 1,000-bed university teaching hospital.

As I continued to work, I completed my MBA in healthcare administration and then began to teach both at the academic level and for the American College of Healthcare Executives. Teaching helped me to better evaluate leadership issues and the human resources positions offered me the chance to see the theories worked out in the real world. Human resources also gave me the best avenue of bringing change to organizations and being involved in all decisions within the organization.

The greatest challenges I faced included the time demands and sacrifices that had to be made in the work/life balance equation and the constantly changing environment. Yet these same challenges provided the complexity and ambiguity that made each day quite stimulating. After twenty years of executive positions, I determined that consulting would provide me with greater insight and breadth in the field. Being a practitioner for so many years also enriched my ability to provide counsel and value in a consulting perspective. Working in the executive search field provides me the opportunity to continue to deal with every aspect of healthcare, from board leadership to financial and physician leadership. My firm, Witt Kieffer, is devoted exclusively to the health field and provides me with many professional partners in the leadership assessment and placement discipline.

The best counsel I could give to new persons entering the field would be to:

- Learn operations and the clinical/patient care aspects of those operations. These are the reasons that healthcare organizations exist.
- Learn how organizations fit together. Although it is easiest to do so by beginning a career in a smaller organization, those new to their career can target rotational assignments in larger organizations as well.
- Learn the unwritten expectations that exist in the field, the "make or break" practices that often are more important than technical or administrative knowledge.
- Become a life-long student of leadership, honing in on what it is, how it is measured, and how it is enhanced.

Those just entering the field need to know that healthcare is a demanding master, often asking for sacrifices that surpass those in other industries. They should be prepared to learn the nature of servant leadership and commit to a calling that requires constant focus on those who are in great need.

Sister Pat Eck, CBS

Chairperson, Board of Directors
Bon Secours Health System, Inc.
Marriottsville, Maryland

B.S., Nursing, Medical College of Virginia
M.S., Nursing, Catholic University of America (Washington, D.C.)
M.H.A., Medical College of Virginia
Diplomate, American College of Healthcare Executives

MY CAREER IN healthcare began when I was a student nurse in a diploma program in Richmond, Virginia, in 1962. I graduated in 1965 and began my professional career as a nurse at the Medical College of Virginia in the operating room. It was during that first year of nursing that I experienced the "call" to religious life, and in September 1966, I entered the Congregation of the Sisters of Bon Secours, whose sole commitment and dedication is to health. For fifteen years, I practiced nursing in various settings.

While I was practicing as a clinical specialist, it became clear to me that I wanted to be in organizational settings where I could influence how care was delivered, so I returned to school and ultimately received my master's degree in health administration in 1981. Since 1981, I have been in administration in some form, but always with an eye and attention to the delivery of healthcare.

In 1985, I returned to Richmond and was employed at St. Mary's Hospital as the chief operating officer. The Bon Secours Health system in Richmond began to expand, and from 1990 through 1997, my responsibilities expanded as we developed the Bon Secours Richmond local delivery system. In 1997, I was asked to assume my current position as chairperson for the Bon Secours Health System, Inc., board of directors. This is a full-time position and includes the mission functions for the health system.

For me, as a healthcare executive and leader of a Catholic religiously sponsored healthcare organization, the major challenge is in leading a ministry in an incredibly complex and competitive business environment. That is the challenge, but it is also the reward. I believe the great majority of people who choose healthcare do so because they want to help others. Serving with others who have a similar value set and hope for the field and are willing to struggle to keep compassion in healthcare is a reward in itself.

I think the best advice I can offer a person who is entering the filed of healthcare administration is to respond to your heart's calling and to prepare yourself at every job opportunity for the next level of advancement. Understanding your own personal value set and having it enhanced within the work environment is critically important. Early in one's career there is excitement and energy in learning and doing new things. Over time it will become important that one's "life's work" can be accomplished in daily work life. Understanding oneself and being accountable for one's actions are essential for the journey.

Mary Ellen Frey

Chief Operating Officer
Jamestown Hospital
Jamestown, North Dakota

B.A., Nursing, Jamestown College (North Dakota)
M.A., Management, University of Mary (North Dakota)
Fellow, American College of Healthcare Executives

I ENTERED THE field of health administration after a long career in a wide variety of nursing positions in a rural acute care hospital. I have always been the type of person who likes variety and is driven by an internal desire to be more and do more.

I began as a staff nurse at Jamestown Hospital in Jamestown, North Dakota. I later became an evening nursing supervisor. I also served as an instructor in the North Dakota State Hospital's licensed practical nurse (LPN) program. In the spring of 1979, I became a clinical instructor at Jamestown College. I was director of education at Jamestown Hospital from 1976 to 1982, before becoming director of the division of professional services. I became executive vice president of Jamestown in 1988, and was named chief operating officer in 1998.

Lifelong learning is one of the concepts I believe in and practice. One can always learn. Learning makes you a deeper thinker and a much more versatile professional. I like to be challenged, and I believe health administration provides both challenge and variety. There is never a dull moment and always a wide variety of issues and professionals that one must learn to collaborate with, whether it's a board member, physician, housekeeper, or nurse. Each person and each issue is individual and unique. Health administration requires a core education and the willingness to learn and be willing to step outside the box.

One of the greatest challenges and rewards as a health service executive is to be of service to the field, to coworkers, and to staff. The change in healthcare is overwhelming, with more information and less time to deal with it, less time to do more. I see myself as a role model, mentor, and coach to my staff. These roles take on a new meaning in today's healthcare arena with the shortages of healthcare workers. The future of our healthcare system lies with the young people who are entering the field, at a time when fewer opportunities exist for those individuals in our healthcare system.

The highest reward for me at the end of the day is when I reflect and can identify that I made a difference in the life of one staff member or one patient. Perhaps I supported the staff or assisted in implementing a more effective method of delivering health services to our patients.

The best advice I can give a person entering the field is to adopt the concept of lifelong learning. Join ACHE and be an active participant—doing so made a difference for me. Adopt a service leadership style. The new workforce is driven by different motivators, and it's important to know them. Get connected to your community through a volunteer organization—that's how you learn about the needs of your community. Raise the bar on your personal and professional development and never give up.

Kevin J. Harlen

Vice President for Professional Services
Washington Hospital Center
Washington, D.C.

B.A., Middlebury College (Vermont)
M.S.P.H., University of North Carolina at Chapel Hill

MY INTEREST IN the health administration field stems from a strong desire to be involved in the patient care process. In 1984, during my senior year at Middlebury College in Vermont, I developed a serious interest in medicine and explored several post-baccalaureate pre-med programs, after receiving my bachelor's degree in history. However, the prospect of spending the next ten years studying to become a physician seemed daunting, especially after I married in 1985 and wanted to start a family. Nevertheless, I remained interested in the healthcare field and focused my efforts on healthcare management. In preparation for graduate school, I returned to Boston and worked as an emergency medical technician, a research assistant at Massachusetts General Hospital, and an administrative assistant at Massachusetts Mental Health Center, Harvard Medical School.

In 1986, I matriculated in the health policy and administration program at the University of North Carolina at Chapel Hill and served as administrative resident at the Moses Cone Hospital in Greensboro, North Carolina. Upon graduation, I joined the executive management team at Bayfront Medical Center, a 517-bed private teaching hospital in St. Petersburg, Florida, as vice president for patient care management.

In 1992, I accepted the position of administrator with ImageAmerica, with responsibility for managing two imaging centers in Birmingham, Alabama. Organizational changes within ImageAmerica resulted in the elimination of my position in 1994. Although the timing was not ideal, I had already decided that my skills and interests were not compatible with the sales-focused requirements of the position.

I focused my job search on hospitals and landed the position of director of radiology and nuclear medicine at Washington Hospital Center in Washington, D.C., a 907-bed tertiary care, private teaching hospital, with revenues of approximately $1.5 billion. Subsequently, I became an administrative director and then assistant vice president. In 1999, I advanced to my current position of vice president for professional services, with responsibility for cardiovascular, surgical, anesthesia, women's, emergency medicine, trauma, imaging, pulmonary, nuclear medicine, rehabilitation, laboratory and pathology, and pharmacy services.

My professional affiliations include the Healthcare Financial Management Association, the American College of Healthcare Executives, the American Hospital Association, and the American Burn Association. I serve on the ACHE Regent's Advisory Council, as a board member of the Washington Regional Transplant Consortium, and as a member of the editorial board of the *Journal of Healthcare Management*.

My biggest challenge has been learning to strike the right balance between work and family. I believe our industry is one of the most complex and being successful takes much energy and time. The rewards, however, are tremendous. Seeing a newborn in the nursery or visiting with a patient prior to discharge following lifesaving open heart surgery are only two ways to witness the positive effect our industry has on individuals' health and quality of life.

I offer two pieces of advice to a person entering this field. First, learn to react creatively to the ever-changing and increasingly complex environment of the healthcare industry. Second, never lose sight of why we're in the business—to take care of the sick in an atmosphere of compassion and high quality service.

Richard J. Henley

Executive Vice President, Chief Operating and Financial Officer
Health Quest
Poughkeepsie, New York

B.A., Economics, City College of New York
M.A., Economics, City College of New York
Fellow, American College of Healthcare Executives
Fellow, Healthcare Financial Management Association

FOLLOWING THE COMPLETION of my joint degree program in 1978, I had the opportunity to join a world-class medical center, Mount Sinai Medical Center, a 1,200-bed academic medical center in New York. I started in a staff capacity as the assistant to the vice president for finance and chief financial officer. During the seven years that I spent at Mount Sinai, I was fortunate to enjoy three rapid promotions, each of them approximately eighteen months apart. The positions I held included director of financial planning, associate director of finance, and director of financial professional services.

In my last position at Mount Sinai, I directed the financial activities of a 350-member faculty practice plan, including accounting, billing, reimbursement, planning, and business development. I was responsible for the planning and implementation of all corporate-wide diversification ventures and managed corporate treasury/investment activities, the insurance program, and auxiliary enterprises.

In 1985, I was recruited to Vassar Brothers Hospital in Poughkeepsie, New York, as vice president for finance and chief financial officer. Following two subsequent promotions, I attained my current position of executive vice president and treasurer for both Vassar

Brothers Hospital and its parent system, Health Quest. In my present position, I serve as chief operating and financial officer for a diversified healthcare system that includes two hospitals, a long-term care facility, and several affiliated entities.

Having started in healthcare immediately following my graduation, I have been fortunate to work in this industry for the past 22 years. Clearly, healthcare presents many challenges, including balancing the missions of not-for-profit organizations with the need to generate a margin in order to invest in new programs and to sustain a financially vibrant organization. I have found the challenge of dealing with a multitude of individuals, from members of boards of directors, medical staff, administrative staff, clinical staff, as well as external parties, to be the most rewarding part of my job. Healthcare is a unique business in that individuals are vulnerable when they need to seek out healthcare services. At the same time, competitive forces necessitate constant vigilance of cost management, new program development, expanding relationships with the medical staff, and offering health promotion in the community.

My joint degree program enabled me to develop a strong foundation in economics and finance, critical for anyone contemplating a career in healthcare administration. My coursework included study in investments, financial analysis, statistical analysis, micro-economics, and macro-economics. In addition to formal academic preparation, I have held faculty appointments in healthcare administration (Baruch College and the Mount Sinai School of Medicine), health sciences (Hunter College), and public administration (New York University).

I would give the following advice to anyone entering the field.

- Do not be misled by the "not-for-profit" nomenclature, as the challenges and rewards of working in the healthcare industry are as significant, if not more so, that those in the "for-profit" sector.
- Develop a strong understanding of finance, as this skill set will be critical in any job you may hold in acute care, ambulatory care, managed care, or post-acute care.
- Immerse yourself in learning all that you can once you enter the work force, as education truly does not end on the conferral of your

degree. Keep current on various healthcare issues by attending conferences and reading voraciously. By doing so, you can assure yourself of being on the cutting edge and offering the greatest value to your organization.

- Get involved in your profession, beyond your specific position, by offering to mentor other healthcare professionals or teaching a class in a graduate program in your community.
- Get professional certification such as Fellowship in the American College of Healthcare Executives or the Healthcare Financial Management Association to distinguish yourself from all the others.
- Volunteer in your community at varied not-for-profit organizations, whether health-related or not, to gain the requisite organizational and communication skills.

R. Edward Howell

Director and Chief Executive Officer
University of Iowa Hospitals and Clinics
Iowa City, Iowa

B.S., Biological Sciences, Muskingum College (Ohio)
M.H.A., The Ohio State University

 I ENTERED HEALTH administration as a second career after working for several years as a high school biology teacher and coach of track, basketball, and football. My attraction to health administration and management was a natural progression of my interests in science, education, and leadership, as well as an intrigue with the robust challenges that leaders in health administration face. To pursue my new career, I returned to school to receive a master's degree in health administration from The Ohio State University.

Early on, I decided to pursue a career in academic health center administration as a natural way to work in an environment that combined my diverse interests in the delivery of high quality patient care with an environment that supported the advancement of medicine through training and research programs. This attraction was largely based on the educational values instilled by my parents, both of whom were educators, and my early career as a secondary school teacher of the sciences. Upon graduation from Ohio State, I served as the first Administrative Fellow at the University of Minnesota Hospitals and Clinics, where I remained in various capacities in operations for almost ten years. In 1986, I was appointed as executive director and chief executive officer

(CEO) of the Medical College of Georgia Hospital and Clinics. Following eight years in that position, I was appointed to my current position as the director and CEO at the University of Iowa Hospitals and Clinics.

Successful administrators possess a unique capacity to address the multitude and variety of challenges that confront healthcare providers simultaneously. Simply stated, I chose my profession because I sought a work life in which no two days are alike. I've been amply rewarded with a career that has required me to constantly retool and grow as a professional. The knowledge, skills, and practice concepts I use daily have literally been relearned since graduate school. This reflects what is arguably the greatest reward of the profession, the fact that it is constantly stimulating. Problems and opportunities abound to provide leadership in a positive manner that has a significant effect on the lives of the staff who work at these centers, the patients who come to receive our care, and the students who receive their training. I find it constantly enriching to work with talented people who wrestle with the real life and death struggles of medicine and the constant probing of young people dedicated to learning the healing arts. I'm often guided by the words of Emerson who described success as follows: "To succeed is to make a difference, whether it is in a garden patch, a small child's smile, or a redeemed social condition." Truly, to have a positive impact on other people's lives is perhaps the finest of professional rewards.

My advice to those entering the field is threefold. Choose your graduate program well; I'm thankful nearly every day that I chose Ohio State. Develop a solid foundation of skills, and know what you want to do with your life. Give strong consideration to completion of a post-graduate residency or fellowship. These programs are vital in the development of executive skills and expertise in organizational operations that you will rely on heavily as your career progresses. Strive for a training program that offers you a personal mentorship. Establishing a relationship of trust and mentorship with a senior executive through your training program is a critical component to your development and future success.

It is vital that you outline the goals of your career and break them down into yearly goals, monthly objectives, and daily tasks. This diligent focus is necessary, understanding that rewards are not gained unless risk is taken. Constantly strive to achieve change yourself. Healthcare is a dynamic profession. Complacency quickly leads to professional obsolescence. Constant and diligent pursuit of self-promoted change is the key to a successful and rewarding career.

Note: Since this profile was written, Ed Howell has taken a new position as vice president and chief executive officer of the University of Virginia Medical Center.

John L. Hummer

Chief Executive Officer
MountainView Regional Medical Center
Las Cruces, New Mexico

B.S., Economics, Kansas State University
M.H.S.A., University of Kansas

 DURING THE 1985 winter recess of my junior year of undergraduate studies, my father, a physician, introduced me to A.B. "Jack" Davis, the chairman and chief executive officer of Wesley Medical Center in Wichita, Kansas. At that time, I was preparing for law school. Mr. Davis, whom I consider to have been a healthcare pioneer, spent an entire day introducing me to the dynamic field of hospital administration. After that day with Mr. Davis, I changed my goal of becoming an attorney and instead pursued a career in hospital administration. This decision was grounded in my own prior hospitalizations, my family's medical roots, and my belief that, unlike in other business or legal careers, I would be given the opportunity to make a positive difference in the lives of a very diverse workforce and, most importantly, in the quality of healthcare for patients.

I completed an undergraduate degree in economics and a master's degree in health services administration. During my graduate studies, I served as an intern at the Scott and White Clinic in Temple, Texas. Following my graduate work, I was an administrative resident at Wesley Medical Center in Wichita. Since that time, I have been an assistant administrator, chief operating officer, and chief executive officer in a number of hospitals throughout the country (Texas, Florida, Louisiana, the District of Columbia, and Nevada). These hospitals have included for-profit and not-for-profit facilities, community hospitals, and academic medical centers in the HCA, UHS, and Triad chains. They have ranged in size from 100 beds to over 500 beds. I am currently leading efforts to develop and build a new regional hospital in southern New Mexico with Triad Hospitals, Inc.

Some of my greatest rewards have been learning from my residency mentors, Jack Davis and Jim Biltz, and from a great physician, my father Lloyd Hummer; serving my country as a commissioned officer in the United Stated Army, Adjutant General Branch; serving on a variety of community and professional association boards; and working with so many talented and creative people in hospitals around the country. I have experienced many challenges in my career, including implementing and leading our hospital's hurricane disaster plan for pre- and post-Hurricane Andrew; leading major improvement efforts in a hospital that resulted in its Accreditation with Commendation by the Joint Commission on Accreditation of Healthcare Organizations; leading efforts at The George Washington University Hospital to convert its ownership status from not-for-profit to for-profit; and negotiating difficult union contracts with nurses. My current position affords me the opportunity to incorporate all my experiences and implement, in concert with employees, physicians, and the community, a positive culture and sound operating philosophy in a new hospital facility.

To someone entering the field, I would give the following advice.

- Stand on principle. Speak up and let your ideas be known.
- Treat everyone in the organization, from the housekeepers to the chief of the medical staff, with the same level of human dignity and respect.
- Get involved in your community. Support the local civic and charitable organizations.
- Surround yourself with bright individuals. Be confident in your abilities.

- Do not take all the credit. Give recognition to those who deserve it.
- Be humble, keep your sense of humor intact, and create an enjoyable working environment for your employees. If they consider their working environment to be of quality, then the patients they serve will receive quality healthcare services.
- Always remember that service comes before self.

Andrew T. Jay

Director, Healthcare Technologies Analyst
First Union Securities
Boston, Massachusetts

B.S., Biology, Rensselaer Polytechnic Institute (New York)
D.M.D., University of Pennsylvania
M.B.A., J.L. Kellogg Graduate School of Management, Northwestern
University (Illinois)

 THE IDEA OF making a contribution to society through healthcare has appealed to me since I was in my teens. This philosophy drew me into patient care and becoming a dentist. Ultimately, however, I moved into management because it allows one to make a larger impact by leveraging the activities of others.

My advanced education began with a dental degree through a combined program with the University of Pennsylvania and Rensselaer Polytechnic Institute in Troy, New York. In this program, I completed my undergraduate degree in two years and was tracked into dental school. This program halved the time to complete my B.S. in biology, eliminated the arduous professional school application process, and guaranteed me admission to a top dental program.

Returning to Boston as a dentist, I acquired a substantial practice through a leveraged buy-out. In the subsequent four years, I more than doubled the size of the practice and increased new patient flow five-fold. Interacting with patients, marketing the practice, and integrating new staff members were particularly enjoyable challenges for me.

It quickly became apparent that my business skills matched or exceeded my skills in dentistry. The business-related challenges were very stimulating. I decided that broadening my background in health services management could expose me to similar challenges on an ongoing basis so I sold my practice and used the proceeds to obtain a M.B.A. at Northwestern's Kellogg School. At Kellogg, my coursework centered on health services management, finance, and marketing. Kellogg provided an excellent foundation for me.

After graduation, I joined Arthur D. Little's Healthcare Delivery Practice. My first consulting assignment was traveling to Saudi Arabia and converting Aramco's healthcare benefits plan from a series of owned and operated clinics to a preferred provider network. This was tremendously satisfying as we improved the quality of care, expanded services, and reduced costs in one sweeping change. I then returned to the United States and completed a variety of consulting assignments including cases in medical devices, pharmaceutical, and healthcare services. Arthur D. Little was an outstanding training ground. However, I felt my knowledge and experience were not being fully used, so I made the transition to Wall Street, becoming a research analyst for medical devices at Alex Brown.

With a colleague, we built one of Wall Street's largest medical device teams, bringing public numerous companies, including Perclose, Wesley Jessen VisionCare, and Xomed. Alex Brown's strength was in working with small to mid-cap growth companies. However, when Deutschebank acquired Alex Brown, the organization lost its small to mid-cap growth stock focus, and I was receptive to recruiters representing First Union Securities who asked me to establish a medical device effort at this emerging powerhouse. First Union's medical device team is widely recognized as the most knowledgeable about innovations involving the brain and spine.

Looking back, my most significant achievement would be the conversion of the health systems at Aramco. This project favorably affected the lives of millions of people. My greatest challenge is my ongoing work with young companies that are bringing lifesaving technologies to market. The healthcare system can be very resistant to change and can be misguided; knee-jerk cost-consciousness has only made this worse!

I encourage those entering health services management to spend time with those who deliver care. Visit an operating room and observe cases, spend a few days in an emergency room, or volunteer in a hospital. These activities will lift your understanding of healthcare delivery astronomically, and your effectiveness in driving change will increase accordingly.

Charles N. (Chip) Kahn

President
Health Insurance Association of America
Washington, D.C.

B.A., Social and Behavioral Sciences/Political Science, The Johns Hopkins University (Maryland)
M.P.H., Health Systems Management, Tulane University (Louisiana)

SINCE 1999, I have been president of the Health Insurance Association of America (HIAA), an influential trade association that represents companies that provide health, long-term care, disability, dental, and supplemental coverage to millions of Americans. My job is to maintain the association's leadership position and to ensure sound and responsible advocacy on legislative and regulatory matters, both in the states and in the nation's capital.

I have long been convinced that to make a difference in people's lives, and to improve the health of the nation, we must have sound public policy. This principle informed my educational choices, as I complemented an undergraduate degree in political science with a graduate degree in public health. Early in my career, I directed the Office of Financial Management Education at the Association of University Programs in Health Administration (AUPHA), after completing an administrative residency with the Teaching Hospital Department of the Association of American Medical Colleges. And, more than 25 years ago, I managed the first two bids for elective office of former Speaker of the House, Newt Gingrich.

In 1983, I began working for Congress as a legislative assistant for health to Senator Dan Quayle (R-IN), then as senior health policy advisor to Senator David Durenburger (R-MN), and then as minority health counsel to the House Ways and Means Committee. From there, I went to HIAA in 1993 and 1994, serving as executive vice president in charge of federal affairs, policy development, research, and communications. During this time, our country debated the pros and cons of the Clinton Administration's proposed healthcare reforms. Under my direction, HIAA raised key questions about these proposals, with a ground-breaking advertising campaign featuring an "ordinary" American couple, Harry and Louise. Returning to "the Hill," I became staff director of the Health Subcommittee of Ways and Means (1995–1998) where I played a role in the passage of the Health Insurance Portability and Accountability Act (HIPAA) and the Medicare provisions of the 1997 Balanced Budget Act (BBA '97).

Despite the pressure-cooker atmosphere of Congress, there is no doubt that my current position is the most challenging one so far. My task is to maintain day-to-day operations of a major organization, while engaging in advocacy that serves both the members and the public. One of my more recent goals has been to focus attention on the uninsured, to place this critical issue on the public policy agenda. The HIAA has commissioned and published key research on the uninsured; earlier this year, I brought back Harry and Louise as advocates for the uninsured, a move applauded even by traditional critics of the industry.

In addition to my work for Congress and HIAA, I have held numerous academic and advisory appointments, have taught health policy, and have written on healthcare financing, recently coauthoring articles in *Health Affairs*.

To anyone entering the field of health administration, I would say that a knowledge of health policy can help you understand why decisions are made and who will be helped or harmed by them. Having this deeper understanding can make the difference between a job and a vocation and can help you steer your own career into perhaps unexpected and rewarding byways.

Note: Since this profile was written, Chip Kahn has left the Health Insurance Association of America and is now the president of the Federation of American Hospitals, an organization representing investor-owned hospitals and healthcare systems.

Laura C. Kayser

Program Officer
American International Health Alliance
Washington, D.C.

B.S.N., Boston College (Massachusetts)
M.P.H., Columbia University (New York)
M.A., International Affairs, Columbia University

 I DEVELOPED AN interest in medicine and public health in my early teens, while volunteering at my local chapter of the American Red Cross. My career goals took shape under the mentorship of a dynamic administrator, who encouraged me to pursue my vision of providing medical care in rural Africa. Several years later, I found these dreams fulfilled, when I flew to a small village in Cote d'Ivoire to serve as coordinator of an integrated rural health project. My bachelor's degree in nursing and several paid and voluntary positions in the health field prepared me for my four years as a Peace Corps volunteer in the Cote d'Ivoire and, later, in Zaire.

In Africa, my commitment to international health was tested and validated, leading me to Columbia University, where I pursued joint master's degrees in international affairs and public health. Following completion of this program, I took a short respite from international work to start a family and become part of a committed corps of public health workers mobilized against the emerging HIV/AIDS epidemic in its epicenter, New York City. As program management officer of the Bureau of AIDS Education, Outreach and Community Development, I coordinated the NYC Health Department's response to the epidemic in high-risk behavior groups, including IV substance users, sex workers, gay men, and inmates. I later worked with the New York State AIDS Institute, developing clinical guidelines for the treatment and prevention of pediatric AIDS.

My husband's career path then took us to Estonia, a former Soviet republic, now an independent Baltic state. Discovering that Estonians had few opportunities for exercise, my first venture there was to establish a western-style fitness club. Once it was operational, I turned my sights back to healthcare and began work for the American International Health Alliance (AIHA). AIHA is a not-for-profit organization dedicated to the belief that American healthcare providers and their communities can make important practical contributions to addressing the healthcare issues that are common to the United States and the former communist countries. AIHA advances global health through volunteer driven partnerships that emphasize economically viable, low-technology solutions to improve productivity and care.

Since 1994, I have grown with AIHA, working first as director for the Baltic Region, then as regional director for Central and Eastern Europe, and, since 1998, as program officer in the Washington, D.C., headquarters office. AIHA's unique approach of uniting American healthcare providers with overseas counterparts allows me to draw on my international background, while keeping abreast of healthcare trends in the United States.

My experience indicates that combining a clinical and management background is very advantageous. My nursing background provided a solid understanding of health systems, resources, and constraints. Those interested in international health should take advantage of international opportunities early in their careers. My Peace Corps experience opened a range of possibilities and each new country has contributed to my understanding of comparative health systems.

The state of global health is critical to our future. Increasingly, America's healthcare experience will have significance for the world's health trouble spots. In response, skilled healthcare managers with insight and compassion will be in great demand.

Narendra M. Kini

Vice President of Clinical and Support Services
Children's Hospital of Wisconsin
Milwaukee, Wisconsin

M.D., University of Lagos (Nigeria)
M.S.H.A., University of Alabama at Birmingham

BORN IN INDIA, I attended medical school at the University of Lagos in Nigeria, West Africa. While pursuing medicine as a career, I knew healthcare management was the area on which I wanted to focus. I chose to get advanced training in health management at the University of Alabama at Birmingham before completing my clinical training at the Medical College of Wisconsin in Milwaukee.

Board certified in pediatrics and in pediatric emergency medicine, I have been an attending physician in the emergency department/ trauma center (ED/TC) at Children's Hospital of Wisconsin since 1992. It has been important, throughout my career, to remain clinically involved with patients and to continue to staff the ED/TC.

After completing a one-year fellowship in health administration, I became administrative director of utilization review and quality assurance at Children's Hospital. Since then, I have held faculty positions at the Medical College of Wisconsin and served as physician advisor to the hospital's quality improvement department, where I worked on utilization management, quality improvement, and managed care contracting.

In 1997, I was appointed vice president of clinical and support services, overseeing the following hospital departments: pharmacy, laboratory, radiology, clinical engineering, facilities, food services, and environmental services. I also am involved in outcomes research and am the medical director for a collaborative project involving a number of pediatric hospitals.

One of my primary interests is international healthcare and how the United States can help developing countries adapt the best features of our healthcare system to meet their needs. It has been proven that simply providing these countries the healthcare system that works for us is not enough.

My main reason for entering health services administration was the desire to help manage health issues across populations. Recognizing the best outcomes are not necessarily related to the most expensive and complex systems, I am also interested in studying different systems to determine an optimal method of managing healthcare, especially in areas with significant resource constraints.

My greatest challenge has been to respond to problems as part of a team, which is the opposite of what clinical training emphasizes, and the major source of conflict between physicians and healthcare managers. My most important skill is obtaining buy-in from groups of constituents with varied backgrounds who offer different perspectives. This is particularly important in a non-clinical area where I had a lot to learn quickly.

My greatest reward has been using my diverse background to serve our customers successfully. Convincing our environmental services staff that their job is as important to patient outcomes as clinical care is an example.

As the healthcare system evolves, it is important to have an operational understanding of advances in medical technology and informatics in order to make sound decisions. Since the system is constantly changing, my advice to anyone entering the field is to find an apprenticeship after completing your formal study. Seek a mentor and focus on the part of the complex system you wish to pursue.

Stephanie M. Lenzner

Business Development, Managed Care
Televox Software, Inc.
Mobile, Alabama

B.S., Public Administration, University of Wisconsin–Green Bay
M.B.A., University of Alabama at Birmingham
M.S.H.A., University of Alabama at Birmingham

 WHILE DIFFICULT TO determine "The Day" I became aware health administration was for me, I did know this: I loved working with people; I desired a career that would allow me to make a difference in people's lives; I wanted a fast-paced career that combined my interests in business, health, and policy; and lastly, I wanted to feel passionate about my work.

When pursuing an undergraduate degree in public administration, my healthcare elective courses appealed to me. I explored these interests through internships with a local health department and a newly integrated provider-owned health system. I worked on multiple outreach projects, conducted research, and lobbied for preventive care funding. I shadowed the executive-vice president of the health system in all finance, executive staff, and board meetings. These internships confirmed my desire to work in healthcare and to continue on for a graduate degree.

After applying, visiting, and being accepted to multiple graduate schools, I decided to further my education at a university where I felt most comfortable with the curriculum, alumni, and professors—The University of Alabama at Birmingham. The program was ranked in the top ten and I felt "at home" in Birmingham. Six months later, I moved from the cold of Wisconsin to the heat of Alabama with no regrets.

While attending graduate school, I was a graduate assistant for the program director and ACHE student chapter president, and I began working part-time for a managed care organization on projects regarding physician behavior and preventive performance. These activities allowed me to apply my classroom learning and to network with individuals playing a vital role in my career. I was offered and accepted a residency with the HMO and was hired for a permanent position in marketing and member communications, considered senior management. After working with many departments including quality, compliance, sales, and operations, I was then promoted to manager of pharmacy benefits.

As manager of pharmacy benefits I found the "niche" I had been searching for. While indirectly, I felt I was helping to improve member health status by drafting communication regarding routine exams and medication compliance. I worked with the contracted pharmacy benefit manager (PBM) to implement a disease management program geared at education and prevention. I felt good about the work I was doing. Therefore, when I was offered a business development position within TeleVox Software to increase prevention and disease management awareness using innovative technology, I jumped at the opportunity.

In my current position, I work with health plans and disease management organizations nationwide to provide cost-effective, personalized reminders for preventive initiatives, such as mammograms, immunizations, and preventive screening exams. I feel more passionate about my work than ever; I respect my coworkers and believe in the mission of our company; I enjoy the commitment to prevention of our clients; and I believe at some level I am making a difference in people's lives.

In my brief career, I feel very blessed for my opportunities and the amazing people I have met. My many mentors have proved invaluable, and I carry a part of them with me every day. I never had any intentions of ending up in the technology industry when I sought a career in healthcare. In fact, I would have laughed if someone had suggested it.

For what it is worth, this early careerist would like to offer the following advice to new persons entering the field: keep an open mind about your career path; do not be afraid to take risks; show initiative by putting yourself in a position to embrace new opportunities; network and surround yourself with mentors you believe in; treat people with respect, remembering your classmates and coworkers are colleagues; make a commitment to lifelong learning; and love your work.

Jean G. Leon

Executive Director
Kings County Hospital Center
Senior Vice President
BSI Family Health Network
Brooklyn, New York

B.S., Health Administration, St. Joseph's College (New York)
M.P.A., New York University

 I AM CURRENTLY the executive director of Kings County Hospital Center and senior vice president of the Brooklyn-Staten Island Family Health Network. I am responsible for the budget of the facilities, for overseeing the entire operations of the facilities, and for ensuring that the best quality of care is rendered to everyone, regardless of the ability to pay. The greatest challenge of my position is adapting, while continuing to improve, the facility to the changing healthcare environment. As the healthcare industry moves from diagnosis-related group reimbursement to managed care, I strive to balance meeting the constantly changing needs of my patients with dwindling financial resources. I am proud that my facility achieved accreditation with commendation in 1997, the first such occurrence in its 169-year existence. The past four years have also seen Kings County Hospital Center operating in the black and making efforts to streamline and re-engineer the organization, while modernizing to meet the growing competition in the marketplace.

I began my career as a registered nurse, but shifted to health administration when I realized that I wanted to have more of an effect on policy and decision making. In addition to my formal education, I hold certification in quality assurance and nursing administration and have lectured and consulted extensively in healthcare. I am a member of the National Association of Health Care Quality and the American College of Healthcare Executives, and have received many awards, including the New York State Quality Assurance Health Care Professional Award in 1995.

I began my tenure with New York's Health and Hospitals Corporation as assistant director of nursing at Woodhull Hospital and Mental Health Center. I then joined Metropolitan Hospital Center as director of quality management, later becoming associate executive director with increasing responsibilities for quality management. Next, I moved to Harlem Hospital Center as deputy executive director, remaining there until I was appointed chief operating officer of Kings County Hospital Center in 1994. Months later, I was promoted to the position I currently hold.

For those considering a career in health administration, I suggest that a commitment to healthcare is a valuable trait to cultivate. This commitment should eventually lead to a good working knowledge of the healthcare industry. I believe that some sort of practical experience in the delivery of care in many ways is a precursor to good policymaking. I also believe it is important to develop a good sense of people management, as well as sharp communication skills.

Wayne M. Lerner

President and Chief Executive Officer
Rehabilitation Institute of Chicago
Chicago, Illinois

B.S., Psychology, University of Illinois
M.H.A., University of Michigan
D.P.H., University of Michigan
Fellow, American College of Healthcare Executives

 UNTIL HOWARD BERMAN, the brother of a close friend introduced me to hospital administration during my senior year in college, I had planned to go to graduate school in clinical psychology. Although I had never even heard of the field, I was interested in talking to him about it because I had great respect for his opinion.

We spent considerable time discussing the profession while I researched it. As someone who had never taken any business or health-related courses, I realized I would be able to gain only a superficial understanding of the field's intricacies, but the attraction was strong. Even though I had no idea about the specifics of the field, I applied to graduate school, and, after a successful interview, was accepted into the graduate health administration program at the University of Michigan.

The first year was spent learning new concepts and improving my basic business skills. I had a mathematics minor, so many of the quantitative courses came relatively easily for me. The summer between my first and second years was spent in an administrative externship at Rush-Presbyterian-St. Luke's Medical Center in Chicago under the tutelage of Gail Warden, a Michigan alumnus who had a wonderful reputation both as an outstanding executive and mentor of students. During that summer that I realized I had made the right career choice; I never looked back or second-guessed my decision.

Following graduation from Michigan, I assumed an administrative position at Rush and spent the next 17 years there. Over that span, I had five different jobs, ranging from ambulatory care administration to medical school administration to being responsible for both the main teaching hospital and the graduate program in health administration. I had many different experiences managing in a variety of settings, each with its own special constituencies, all of which were critical to the success of the enterprise.

About five years into my career at Rush, it became clear to me that I should pursue advanced educational opportunities. I investigated attending law school or a doctoral program in a related field. Luckily, the Pew Charitable Trust had decided to fund an experiment in practitioner doctoral education, and I was fortunate enough to be admitted into the first class, again at Michigan, and graduated four years later with a doctor of public health degree with a concentration in health policy. Those years, the individuals I met at Michigan and the other Pew programs, and the intensive interactions with faculty made an indelible mark on me. Not only was I more convinced then ever that I had made the correct career choice, but also now had more options to pursue within the field than ever before.

I left Rush in 1990 to become president of The Jewish Hospital of St. Louis. During the six years I was in St. Louis, we not only created one of the largest hospital systems in the nation (BJC Health System) but also merged the two adult teaching hospitals to create one of the most respected institutions in the country, Barnes-Jewish Hospital. I learned a tremendous amount in a new community working to create the first integrated system in that area and managing the intricacies involved. In addition, I was able to join Washington University as a faculty member in its health administration program.

After merging myself (purposely) out of a job, I returned to Chicago in a consulting role, reacquainting myself with my family. Seven months later, an executive search consultant for the Rehabilitation Institute of Chicago (RIC) called me looking for individuals who might be interested in the chief executive officer role. Because RIC had a wonderful reputation, and it sounded like the talents I had would fit well with the needs of the organization, I pursued the job with great interest.

After almost five years at RIC, I can again say that I made the correct choice. The greatest challenges I face include balancing healthcare's social mission with sound business practice, motivating staff and the management team to meet the organization's mission while being cognizant of the economic pressures upon us, and maintaining some sort of balance between my professional and personal life. This is probably the most difficult aspect of a healthcare executive's life.

The rewards have been plentiful. It has brought me great joy to mentor students and staff. It is exhilarating to see the accomplishments of your staff in implementing changes to improve service and quality and to meet the business requirements of the field. It is personally rewarding to be a part of the policy development process and see your input in either new legislation or regulation. The best rewards, however, are when I visit patients and see the fruits of all our labors making a positive impact on a person's life. After all, that is why we chose this field. And, I have been able to continue my interest in teaching as a member of Northwestern Kellogg Graduate School of Management faculty.

Organizations require the talents and skills of many different people. Working with such heterogeneous groups is not only fun but should be considered part of the learning and growing process, as well. Healthcare leadership has to be one of the most complex, demanding professions one could possibly imagine. Every day, you need to remember what you have learned that day and how you can put it into practice tomorrow. People's lives depend on you and your decisions, and current and future patients will look to you for guidance and support. If you want to integrate organizational skills with an overriding social concern—and believe that organizational leadership derives primarily from the character, values, and persona of leaders—then this is the right field for you.

Lisa A. Macus, Major, United States Air Force

Senior Program Analyst, Financial Management Directorate
Office of the Surgeon General of the U.S. Air Force
Washington, D.C.

B.S., Health Planning and Administration, Pennsylvania State University
M.B.A., Arizona State University
M.H.S.A., Arizona State University
Diplomate, American College of Healthcare Executives

 I WAS ONE of the few high school students who took her career aptitude test seriously. Fortunately for me, hospital administration ranked at the top of my list. I had originally planned to major in engineering or business, as my strengths were the quantitative disciplines of math and science. However, as college drew closer the "people" and "caregiving" aspects of hospital administration piqued my interest. I graduated from Pennsylvania State University with a bachelor's of science in health planning and administration, with a minor in business administration. After graduation, I immediately joined the Air Force. After five years as a department head in various military treatment facilities, the Air Force sponsored me for dual master's degrees at Arizona State University, where I earned a master's degree in business administration (MBA) and a master's degree in health services administration (MHSA).

Many members of my family were shocked when I told them of my decision to join the Air Force. After four years of college they didn't understand why I chose to begin my career in the military. Today, they have completely changed their opinions and would be upset if I left the Air Force. I discovered the opportunities the Air Force offered while at Penn State, when I saw a brochure on the bulletin board advertising, "Run your own department and receive training." As a 20-year old, this appealed to me, because the job market was not as lucrative in 1988 as it is today. I thought this would be a perfect job in which to gain some experience for three years. I had no desire to be a research assistant or a glorified "gopher." When I graduated, few employers were hiring people with limited experience. After extensive research, I realized the Air Force and I would be a good match, and I have yet to be disappointed. I got what was promised and so much more.

At 21, I ran the patient administration department at Whiteman Air Force Base, Missouri. At the time, I had about eight staff members reporting to me. I went on to become the director of medical logistics management, where I had 16 staff members under my charge. After four years, I made a lateral move to Andersen Air Force Base in Guam and gained experience as the director of medical readiness.

After graduate school, I was stationed in San Diego at the Naval Medical Center, working for the Office of the Lead Agent, TRICARE Southern California. Here I was the chief of marketing, where my primary duties included acting as the liaison between the managed care support contractor and the government on all marketing and education matters. After three years, I transferred to Washington, D.C., to my current position as a senior program analyst in the Financial Management Directorate of the Office of the Surgeon General, Headquarters, U.S. Air Force. In this role, I am responsible for the planning, management, and execution of the Air Force Medical Service's $1.3 billion budget. To date, working on the Air Force Surgeon General's staff has been the most difficult yet most rewarding assignment.

My greatest challenge was adapting to the cost-competitive, for-profit environment that overrides today's healthcare system. Although I don't see the harsh effects I might encounter in the private sector, it is apparent that today's healthcare environment is not the caring, compassionate field I had aspired to work in when I began my career. It is much more competitive and dollar-driven than I imagined, but I've discovered there is a place for patient rights, empathy, and compassion in the healthcare field.

Working as an Air Force healthcare administrator has been a rewarding career choice. My dual roles as an Air Force officer and healthcare administrator have given me the opportunity to travel the world and to work with some of the most talented individuals I have ever met. A tremendous bond is often created with the people one meets and serves with, and many of these bonds last a lifetime. If I had to do it over again, there is little I would change about my career. I have been fortunate to serve my country as an Air Force healthcare administrator.

Note: Since this profile was written, Lisa Macus has become the Business Operations and Beneficiary Services Flight Commander at Nellis Air Force Base in Nevada. She has also recently married and is now Lisa Beck.

Mary K. Mologne

Director, Quality and Accountability Initiatives
American Hospital Association
Washington, D.C.

B.S., Health Policy and Management, The Pennsylvania State University
M.B.A., Fuqua School of Business, Duke University (North Carolina)
Diplomate, American College of Healthcare Executives

GROWING UP THE daughter of a surgeon and hospital administrator, I was exposed early in my life to the fields of medicine and healthcare management. I debated early in my education about attending medical school and was excited to learn about the undergraduate degree in health administration, which in my mind, married the best of both worlds and would be a better fit with my skill sets. Not knowing exactly what I wanted to become, I realized quickly that the healthcare field provided a growing, ever changing environment, within which to experiment and crystallize my career desires and goals.

I declared my major as health policy and administration at The Pennsylvania State University and began my healthcare career journey. The degree provided a unique mix of lessons in business, policy, and social sciences; it tested both my analytical and creative sides and gave me exposure to clinical and ethical curricula.

My degree also provided the opportunity to practice these lessons in a valuable internship. I was fortunate to complete this internship at the George Washington University Medical Center, which gave me my first true exposure to the field I had chosen. More than any specific experiences that summer, I developed relationships with mentors who opened doors to many other mentors and opportunities. While he was writing my reference letter for acceptance into graduate school, one of those mentors, an assistant administrator at the medical center, told me about an opportunity at the District of Columbia Hospital Association (DCHA). After exploration, I decided to pull my application from graduate school and join the DCHA staff.

The DCHA provided one of the broadest exposures to our healthcare system. It allowed me to participate firsthand in policymaking at the national and local levels. And, as a general project manager, my roles exposed me to virtually every part of healthcare, from disaster preparedness to hospital—medical staff relations to culturally sensitive communication with patients.

While my undergraduate education had prepared me for these roles exceptionally well, I quickly learned of my degree's limitation, and decided to complement it with an MBA and health services management concentration from the Fuqua School of Business at Duke University. These fabulous two years broadened my perspective of healthcare, taught me new skills and business discipline to apply to my healthcare knowledge, and strengthened my network of healthcare leaders.

From Duke, I moved on to the SunHealth Alliance as an administrative resident, again broadening my network of contacts and mentors and gaining new exposures in healthcare management. I held various roles at SunHealth and later with Premier, Inc. (after merger), including managed care and strategic consultant and regional executive. These organizations provided a perfect environment to mix my healthcare and business skills.

Four years later, the American Hospital Association asked me to join its staff as director of quality and accountability, my current position. As such, I am responsible for the development, implementation, and management of products and services to improve patient care and enhance public confidence and trust in hospitals and health systems. Two primary areas of focus are on improving patient safety by reducing/preventing medication errors and improving care at the end of life in hospitals and health systems.

My biggest professional challenge has been establishing credibility in the field of clinical quality improvement without having a clinical degree, but I have found that it can be done! Counting among my colleagues, mentors, and friends so many passionate, mission-driven leaders in our field has been my greatest professional reward.

I would give the following advice to someone entering the field.

- Seek out mentorship opportunities as often as possible. Network, network, network, and follow through with those you meet. I have countless examples (as recent as this year!) of the power of a handwritten note of thanks.
- Seek out opportunities to interact with executive audiences in the field, at school functions, internships and other employment situations, and other social or alumni functions. Avoid being intimidated by their positions of authority, and realize that most are very approachable and welcome the opportunity to teach you and even learn from you. As I've noted throughout this message, our field has been characterized by strong mentorship relationships, relationships that are not often forgotten and that make lasting impressions to carry on the tradition.
- Be flexible and learn to embrace change. A positive, adaptable spirit and personality are received with open arms in this ever-changing environment. Learn to thrive on ambiguity!
- Strike an appropriate balance between being a generalist and a specialist. It never hurts to be viewed as an expert in an area, but to have a basic depth of knowledge on the broadest of healthcare issues will facilitate your flexibility and adaptability to change.

Note: Since this profile was written, Mary Mologne has left the AHA and is now senior product manager with PYXIS, a Cardinal Health company.

Robert W. Omer

President and Chief Executive Officer
MCH Health System
Blair, Nebraska

B.S., Biology, University of Utah
M.H.A., Washington University (Missouri)
Fellow, American College of Healthcare Executives

WHILE I WAS an undergraduate student at the University of Utah, I had the opportunity to work in clinical healthcare delivery in a large regional hospital. It was there that I was first exposed to the management of healthcare organizations. I knew then that I had found the ideal way of working with people to serve people. I went on to take a master of health administration degree at Washington University in St. Louis and to complete a nine-month hospital residency.

Over the years, I have held six administrative positions. I began as associate administrator for General Services at St. Luke's Hospital in Cedar Rapids, Iowa, a 620-bed institution. I served there for five years. I then moved to Franciscan Medical Center in Rock Island, Illinois, serving as assistant administrator for medical services. After five years, I became vice president of 520-bed LDS Hospital in Salt Lake City, Utah.

After three years at LDS Hospital, I became vice president and chief operating officer at Bishop Clarkson Memorial Hospital, and, after twelve years, chief executive officer of the Heartlands Clinics, a nine clinic network, both in Omaha, Nebraska. I am now president and chief executive officer of Memorial Community Hospital and Health

System in Blair, Nebraska, a small community about 20 miles from Omaha. The system includes the hospital, three primary care clinics, and a home health agency.

I have also pursued a second career in military medicine. My service began as a college student in the Army Reserve Officer Training Corp. I was commissioned in 1972 and assigned to the Medical Service Corp—the Army's healthcare administration cadre. Over a period of 26 years, I served in a variety of hospital and medical units, including the modern version of the "MASH" mobile field hospital. In 1991, I was called to active duty during Operation Desert Storm, serving at Fort Belvoir, Virginia, as the Chief of Plans, Training, Mobilization, and Security at DeWitt Army Hospital. My duties included coordinating with all of the military and civilian hospitals in Northern Virginia and the District of Columbia.

I graduated from the Army Command and General Staff College, Fort Leavenworth, Kansas, and I was awarded the Army Commendation Medal and the Army Achievement Medal. I retired as a lieutenant colonel.

I joined the American College of Hospital Administrators as a graduate student in 1973 and have benefited as a member throughout my career. I advanced in the College by successfully completing the Governors Examination. I then continued my advancement to Fellow, the highest category of membership. I have had many opportunities to serve the College, which became the American College of Healthcare Executives (ACHE). I served as president of the Heartland Healthcare Executive Group in 1990, and served on the ACHE Public Policy Committee from 1993 to 1996. In 1997, I was elected ACHE Regent for Nebraska, representing over 200 affiliates to the College for four years. This year I was honored with the 2001 Career Achievement Award for ACHE in Nebraska. ACHE membership has been invaluable, both in networking, executive searches, and continuing education in the field.

My greatest challenges and rewards have come from creating teamwork among providers, employees, volunteers, trustees, and communities to define and meet healthcare needs. Throughout my career in senior management positions, I have had the opportunity to orchestrate the development of new services, facilities, and work teams to meet the needs of the patients we are committed to serve. Working in health services administration has given me the opportunity to develop leadership skills, and to serve in many hospitals, associations, community groups, and professional societies.

My advice to an entry-level manager would be to commit to excellence in all you do and to be proactive in working with superiors, peers, and subordinates. You must realize that healthcare administration requires a commitment to life-long learning. I would encourage a young manager to volunteer for projects, assignments, and opportunities to learn and to be involved. Health services administration is a dynamic and challenging field, with great rewards for those committed to serve others.

Note: Since this profile was written, Mr. Omer has accepted the position of chief executive officer at Cooper County Memorial Hospital and Clinics in Boonville, Missouri. Cooper County Memorial Hospital and Clinics is affiliated with University of Missouri Health Care in Columbia.

Judith C. Pelham

President and Chief Executive Officer
Trinity Health
Novi, Michigan

B.A., Government and International Relations, Smith College (Massachusetts)
M.P.A., Harvard University (Massachusetts)
Fellow, American College of Healthcare Executives

AFTER SEVERAL YEARS of work in government as a consultant, I became all too familiar with the shortcomings of Medicare and Medicaid. The experience left an indelible impression. The programs didn't work well from the standpoint of cost or improving access to care for people. So, I turned my passion toward a career in healthcare administration, because I wanted to change healthcare and the way it was delivered.

In preparing to manage those changes, I sought a graduate school that taught both business skills and provided lessons in ground breaking healthcare administration. At Harvard, I was allowed to develop my own degree. I took half of my classes from the world-renowned Harvard Business School and the rest from the university's School of Public Health and other programs. Each semester included an independent study, during which I served as apprentice to an administrator leading change in the healthcare field.

I put those lessons to work immediately after graduation in 1975. In my first job, with an inner-city health center in Boston, I redesigned the clinic's service strategy after completing a community needs assessment—a novel idea at the time. A year later, I joined Brigham and Women's Hospital in Boston, where I helped create a team-based approach to residency training in primary care internal medicine, a program later to become a national model. In 1981, I moved to the Daughters of Charity system in Austin, Texas, assuming the role of president and chief executive officer at Seton Medical Center a year later. There I developed outreach programs to address the healthcare needs of Hispanics and others. I also laid the groundwork for an integrated delivery network through the provision of new tertiary and home health services for Central Texas.

I had very important early influences that became themes for the rest of my career. I was continually challenged to improve access to services for the poor and to reach out and understand community healthcare needs. At the same time, there was the ever-present challenge to improve the quality of care, while doing so in a cost-effective way.

In 1993 I moved to Mercy Health Services of Farmington Hills, Michigan, to become president and chief executive officer of the 20-hospital system. There, I worked to support the creation of integrated delivery networks across the system's markets. I shepherded the system through tumultuous financial times (stemming from the 1997 Balanced Budget Act) and the vagaries of managed care. Most recently, I oversaw the consolidation of Mercy and Holy Cross Health System into Trinity Health.

Through it all, I have stayed true to my passion. I advise students in the field to do the same, regardless of life's twists and turns. Be flexible; don't think every step on the career path has to be a step "up." There are some very useful zig-zags between staff work and operations that will give you a broader skill base and ultimately make you a more effective executive.

Lee H. Perlman

President
GNYHA Ventures, Inc.
Subsidiary of Greater New York Hospital Association
New York, New York

B.A., Psychology, Binghamton University (New York)
M.B.A., Johnson Graduate School of Management, Cornell University (New York)
Fellow, American College of Healthcare Executives

WHILE GROWING UP in Forest Hills, New York, I often looked after my father, who battled the lingering effects of rheumatic fever. One night when I was a young teenager, my father became terribly ill and we rushed him to the hospital. I searched the hospital halls for my father's doctor, only to hit one roadblock after another. Later that night my father died, never having received the medical attention he needed. I have always felt that he died from an administrative snafu. After this experience, I vowed to find out how hospitals were managed.

While in high school, I volunteered in a local nursing home, so I could see how healthcare was managed from the inside. I loved working there and must have worked 60 hours a week.

After graduating from Binghamton University in 1980, I received a scholarship to attend Cornell University's business school, where I earned an MBA in health services administration in 1982. Following graduate school, I completed an administrative residency at Long Island Jewish Medical Center and then joined the Greater New York Hospital Association (GNYHA) in 1983 as a policy analyst, and I have been here ever since. I have held increasingly responsible positions in health policy development and management of the association's for-profit subsidiaries. I am currently responsible for the growth of the subsidiary's new and innovative businesses that serve the healthcare community and simplify and enhance services for both patients and providers.

In 1996, I launched the relationship between GNYHA Services Group Purchasing and Pharmaceutical Group Purchasing Programs and Premier, Inc., one of the largest national group purchasing programs in the country. Under this successful partnership that covers over $1.5 billion in purchasing volume, GNYHA Services acts as the marketing and service arm of Premier in the New York metropolitan and suburban areas. I am also responsible for the creation of Innovatix, the fastest growing alternate care purchasing group in the nation. Group purchasing creates dollar savings that can be used for patient care.

I am now heavily involved in the management of the association's businesses and affairs, and I continue to be involved in its advocacy agenda as well. A lot of the energy I need to do the business side of my job comes from the policy side. I don't think you can separate the two. I have been the chief coordinator of several major advocacy events and campaigns, including a rally in defense of Medicare and Medicaid funding in Times Square in 1995. Over 20,00 people attended, and Hillary Clinton was the featured speaker. I have also been involved in campaigns seeking coverage for the 40 million Americans without health insurance.

Volunteering is an important part of my life. I currently serve as an active board member for the Institute for Diversity in Health Management and as chairman of the Shorefront Young Men's–Young Women's Hebrew Association of Brighton Beach in Brooklyn, where I have helped coordinate education and job training services for Jewish refugees from the former Soviet Union. I am the founder and organizer of an annual clothing drive and Christmas dinner to help the homeless at the YWCA in Brooklyn. I am the vice president of the Binghamton University Alumni Association and have served on its board of directors since 1994, and I am past president of the Metropolitan Health Administrators Association.

In 1998, I was fortunate enough to have been selected as the Young Healthcare Executive of the Year by the American College of Healthcare Executives—I was the first trade association executive to be chosen for this honor. As an ACHE Fellow, I currently serve as the Governor for District 1, representing ACHE affiliates in the Atlantic Provinces, Connecticut, Maine, Massachusetts, New Hampshire, New York, Ontario, Quebec, Rhode Island, and Vermont. Prior to this, I served as Regent for New York–Manhattan Bronx.

I have given the following pieces of advice to people entering the field:

- You have to want to be a leader, and your desire for leadership has to be reflected in your personality and demeanor.
- Be willing to start small; volunteer to do the "dirty work."
- Take chances and do not be afraid to express a controversial opinion.
- Think "outside the box."
- Be able to admit when you do not know the answer and be willing to learn.
- Your leadership skills must be continually developed and strengthened at every stage of your career.
- Find a mentor; learning for other leaders is very important.
- Focus on what is right or wrong, not on others' perception of your actions.
- Become active in professional organizations.
- Remember that the world does not owe you anything.
- Always follow up a meeting with a thank you note.
- Be aware of current trends and world events.
- Be a community leader.
- Become a change agent.

Lucien B. Perry

Business Consultant
Arthur Andersen LLP
Atlanta, Georgia

B.S., Management, University of New Orleans (Louisiana)
M.B.A., University of Alabama at Birmingham
M.S.H.A., University of Alabama at Birmingham

 MY INTEREST IN the field of healthcare began while working for a non-profit organization that served as an umbrella agency for the homeless service providers in the city of New Orleans. I wanted to enter the healthcare industry because I wanted to be a part of, and one day lead, the efforts of providing improved healthcare services in the communities in which I live. I applied to and attended the University of Alabama at Birmingham to pursue my master of science in health administration and my MBA. After receiving my MBA in June 1999, I pursued an administrative residency in health administration, a requirement for the MSHA degree, at Saint Joseph's Hospital in Atlanta (SJHA), Georgia, under the guidance of my preceptor, Brue Chandler, SJHA's president. After my residency was completed, I was retained for project work in internal auditing for approximately six months before accepting a position as a business consultant in the healthcare division of Arthur Andersen LLP in December of 2000.

My greatest challenge and reward as a healthcare executive occurred during my administrative residency at Saint Joseph's Hospital of Atlanta. One of my residency experiences was to participate in the Joint Commission on Accreditation of Healthcare Organizations

(JCAHO) Survey. Six months into my residency and six weeks before our survey, the director of food services resigned, and the food services department was the area with the most concerns. My preceptor placed me as interim director of the department and asked me to assist the department's managers during the survey process. The challenge of managing a department through this survey was something I had to face head-on. My inexperience as a department manager was relieved by constant and effective communication between staff and myself. The hard work, great attitudes, and collective efforts of the food services staff resulted in the department shining throughout the survey with great results and no significant problem areas. This experience will serve as my personal reinforcement of hard work whenever I find myself faced with a difficult challenge.

I have two pieces of advice for someone entering the healthcare field. First, get accustomed to continuous research and the constant reading of healthcare materials. Subscribe to healthcare journals, such as *Healthcare Executive*, and make it a daily habit to pick up a newspaper (*USA Today*, *Wall Street Journal*, *Washington Post*, *New York Times*) and read what is going on in the field of business, particularly healthcare. Because the industry is constantly changing, it is very important to be up to date on what is going on. Second, understand that there are no definite answers in the field of healthcare. Healthcare executives who think "outside of the box" will be the executives who succeed. Do not be afraid to ask questions and provide ideas that may even seem a bit unorthodox. The only bad idea is one that is not shared.

In closing, the healthcare industry has provided me with diverse experiences early on in my career, and I look forward to the challenges that lie ahead. It is my intention to realize lessons learned in all of my experiences and attempt to provide the best healthcare services to the communities in which I serve.

Diane Peterson

President
D. Peterson & Associates
Houston, Texas

B.S., Biology. Chatham College (Pennsylvania)
M.P.H., University of Pittsburgh (Pennsylvania)
Fellow, American College of Healthcare Executives

AS A BUDDING scientist, my first job was as a research assistant for the chairman of the biology department at the University of Pittsburgh. I managed his laboratory, research studies, grant applications, and staff, while attending graduate school in human genetics on a part-time basis. I soon realized that I enjoyed management far more than bench research. Instead of writing a thesis in genetics, I switched graduate studies to the health services administration program.

My first hospital employer was Sewickley Valley Hospital in Sewickley, Pennsylvania, a community hospital with ambulatory centers near Pittsburgh. I focused on line operations from resident through vice president of the organization. But, in 1982, for an aspiring female executive, there were few opportunities for a chief executive officer position.

In 1982, I branched off from operations to take a vice president's position in corporate marketing and business development with the Memorial Healthcare System in Houston, Texas. I went from the familiarity of my previous position, friends, and family to start out alone in the Lone Star state. Not only did I have to become a professional marketer—without the benefit of a marketing course—I also had to learn about Houston's unique healthcare environment. Houston healthcare was unbridled by certificate-of-need legislation and fueled by growth, oil, and world-class physicians. Everything was bigger in Texas; yet, I also learned about developing a regional system of tiny, struggling rural hospitals. I worked endless hours committed to building the size and success of the Memorial system.

In 1986, St. Luke's Episcopal Hospital and the Texas Heart Institute in Houston recruited me to become executive vice president for corporate development. It was my first exposure to academic medicine, international healthcare, and professionals such as Denton Cooley, M.D. On one hand, it was enlightening to see research, teaching, and patient care under one roof. On the other hand, it was daunting to grasp the complexities of medical schools' agendas, research grant requirements, departmental chairs' powers, and the competitive pressure of the Texas Medical Center—after all, Dr. DeBakey practiced next door.

But I did not stay long at St. Luke's; the boss and I parted ways after one year. I did not want to place the control of my career in the hands of others, so I opened my own firm.

In 1987, I opened D. Peterson & Associates to provide consulting services to hospitals in the areas of marketing and strategic planning. After years of enjoying executive salaries and perquisites, I was thrilled to make $10,000 profit in my first year of business. The firm has grown and expanded to focus on strategic planning, interim management, and customer service. We have served clients in 26 states and one foreign country.

Throughout all phases of my professional life—line operations, staff support, entrepreneur—the American College of Healthcare Executives has been my professional organization. The College has provided continuing education, a code of ethics, and collegial networking throughout my career. In 2001, I became chairman of the Board of Governors, after serving as a Regent-at-Large and then Governor-at-Large. I am the second woman to serve as chairman; the first was Jesse J. Turnbull, Superintendent of MaGee Women's Hospital in Pittsburgh. I was born in her hospital, under her administration, in 1949—the year she served as chairman of the College!

My advice to all who enter healthcare management is to remain flexible, to mentor others, and to persevere. Flexibility is required in career development and in complex organizations. If you are brittle, you cannot adapt to change or mold to fit new opportunities. Also, healthcare is an industry based upon service to others. Remember to maintain mentoring relationships and to serve your colleagues, in addition to your patients or clients. Finally, perseverance is required in an industry hounded by government regulations, complex challenges, and budget constraints. If you give up too readily, you do not have the stamina for leadership, especially in healthcare. But if you persevere, there is no more satisfying career and life purpose than to be a leader in healthcare.

Janet E. Porter

Associate Dean
School of Public Health
University of North Carolina at Chapel Hill

B.S., Biology, The Ohio State University
M.H.A., The Ohio State University
M.B.A., University of Minnesota
Ph.D., Health Services Research, Policy, and Administration,
University of Minnesota
Diplomate, American College of Healthcare Executives

 IT IS NOT surprising that a college counselor recommended hospital administration as a career, given that my mother is a nurse and my father was in management, and I had been volunteering in hospitals since the age of 13. I had never thought of hospital administration until the aptitude and interest tests administered by the career office at Ohio State University (OSU), as interpreted by their counselor, highlighted it as an option for me.

I chose the OSU MHA program because it offered practical application with a theoretical foundation. My summer residency at Rush—Presbyterian—St. Luke's Medical Center in Chicago reaffirmed my interest in hospital administration. I spent the next five years working as a hospital administrator in Chicago and Ohio.

A brief teaching experience at OSU sparked my interest in earning a Ph.D., and I chose to attend the University of Minnesota because it afforded doctoral students the opportunity to teach. After five years at Minnesota, I had earned an MBA and became a doctoral candidate. My primary interest then was to apply these models and skills in as many organizations as possible. After a brief consulting career with The Lash Group in Washington, D.C., I was recruited back to Ohio to serve as chief operating officer at Children's Hospital, where I worked for nine years. During my tenure at Children's, I taught the strategic management course in the OSU MHA program and also served for two years as a fellow with the Accrediting Commission on Education for Health Services Administration (ACEHSA).

When my husband decided to retire, I accepted a position as CEO of a hospital in Texas. Within nine weeks I resigned as CEO, returning to Columbus unemployed. I was fortunate to be able to work out of OSU's MHA program, teaching, consulting, and seeking full-time employment.

Just as I was deciding to join the faculty at the University of North Carolina (UNC) at Chapel Hill, I was offered the opportunity to lead the Association of University Programs in Health Administration (AUPHA) through a one-year reengineering effort and the search for a permanent president. For the past three years, I have served as a faculty member, teaching the capstone course in the health policy and administration program, and serving as associate dean for executive education for the School of Public Health.

Healthcare administration is gratifying because you can make a real difference in the manner in which patient care is delivered— through management, consulting, or teaching. The best advice I can give anyone regarding a career choice is to find something you love to do so much that you would volunteer to do it, and then find someone who will pay you to do it. I am fortunate to be paid to teach when my passion for teaching is so great that I did it for free for years.

Lawrence D. Prybil

Professor and Associate Dean
College of Public Health
The University of Iowa
Iowa City, Iowa

B.A., Liberal Arts, State University of Iowa
M.A., Hospital and Health Administration, State University of Iowa
Ph.D., Hospital and Health Administration, The University of Iowa
Fellow, American College of Healthcare Executives

AS AN UNDERGRADUATE, I explored several career pathways, including economics, government, and law with a desire to select a field combining public service and organizational leadership. Two of my friends were accepted into graduate programs in health administration and I recall their excitement about the profession. My curiosity led me to conversations with Gerhard Hartman, the director of the University of Iowa Hospitals and Clinics and chairman of the university's graduate program in hospital and health administration. He suggested some readings and encouraged me to visit clinicians and executives in other healthcare institutions. We discussed health and medical care; the economic, social, and technological developments that would transform healthcare; and the challenges healthcare executives face.

I realized that health administration offered enormous opportunities and entered The University of Iowa's graduate program in hospital and health administration in the fall of 1962. I shall always be grateful to Dr. Hartman for taking time, in the midst of busy days, to talk with me. In later years, I realized that commitment to teaching and mentorship is a hallmark of great leaders.

After graduating in 1964, I served a residency at The Jewish Hospital of Saint Louis and, subsequently, three years of active duty in the U.S. Air Force Medical Service.

Nearing the end of my military obligation, several different opportunities became available: assistant administrator positions in Vermont and Connecticut; a job in the U.S. Department of Health, Education, and Welfare; and invitations to pursue doctoral studies. My wife Marilyn and I decided to return to Iowa City and enter the College of Medicine's doctoral program in hospital and health services administration. We felt a doctorate would provide knowledge and skills and create a broader range of possibilities in the future.

In 1970, I completed doctoral studies and accepted a faculty position in at Medical College of Virginia—Virginia Commonwealth University. In 1972, I was asked to become department chairman. For the next eight years, we built a strong faculty and good relationships with the practice community, strengthened the master's degree program, developed a broad-based program of continuing education, and laid the foundation for a doctoral program. I also served for several years as the deputy assistant provost for administration.

Over the years I developed a growing interest in faith-based healthcare services while serving on the board of directors of St. Mary's Hospital in Richmond. In 1980, I accepted an offer from the Sisters of Mercy Health Corporation (SMHC) based in Farmington Hills, Michigan to become the vice president for administration, with responsibility for several corporate functions, including strategic planning, human resources, medical and nursing affairs, quality assurance, and information services. While at SMHC, I also taught one course each year in the graduate health program in health services administration at the University of Michigan.

In 1984, the Daughters of Charity were organizing their healthcare facilities into regional systems with a national service center in St. Louis, Missouri, and I was invited to join that ministry as chief operating officer (COO) for their east-central United States region. As executive vice president and COO of Daughters of Charity National Health System-East Central (DCNHS-EC), I was responsible for the operations of facilities and services in communities in six states. My role included participation at the national level as a member of the DCNHS management council. In 1987, I was named regional executive and chief executive officer of DCNHS-EC and served in that capacity for nearly ten years.

Helping to build a faith-based system from the "ground floor" truly was the experience of a lifetime. Late in 1996, the Daughters concluded it was time to create a new vision and organizational model. I was invited to become a DCNHS national officer and participate in the process of shaping this vision and restructuring the organization. Doing so involved relocation back to St. Louis from Indiana and created the opportunity to affiliate with Saint Louis University and its Center for Health Care Ethics. My responsibilities as a DCNHS senior vice president—which included guiding the consolidation of several regional systems into a unified corporate structure—were challenging, but I enjoyed the opportunity to shape the system's future direction.

In 1999, the opportunity to return home to Iowa appeared when The University of Iowa created the College of Public Health and invited me to return as assistant dean and professor of health management and policy. In July 2000, my title was changed to associate dean for external relations. I oversee development activities, including alumni relations, fund-raising, planning, and the college's external advisory board. I also teach graduate seminars in leadership and healthcare ethics.

As I reflect upon my experiences, I see three continuing challenges. First is the challenge of seeking a good balance among professional and personal responsibilities. One must set priorities, preserve time for your family and personal development, and contribute to community and professional organizations. Searching for the right balance is a life-long journey. A second challenge is the continuous development of knowledge and skills. Healthcare organizations have been remiss in developing high-caliber executive development and leadership succession plans; however, each of us must take personal responsibility for our own development. Finally, in the midst of resource constraints, we must remember that healthcare organizations exist to improve the health of the individuals, families, and communities we serve. We are stewards of organizations whose social role is to serve people and must keep this prominent in our decision-making processes.

My advice to anyone entering the field is to associate with organizations that have clearly stated missions and values, leaders of great integrity, and high standards of conduct. Make a commitment to high standards of performance and ethics, and never compromise them.

Jose B. Quintana

Assistant Professor
Department of Health Services Administration
University of Alabama at Birmingham
Birmingham, Alabama
Acute Care Manager, Surgical Service
VA Medical Center
Birmingham, Alabama

B.S.B.A., Accounting, University of Florida
M.H.A., Duke University (North Carolina)
Ph.D., Administration–Health Services, University of Alabama at Birmingham
Fellow, American College of Healthcare Executives

 I NEVER CONSIDERED health administration as a career option. I was going to be an accountant. The U.S. Air Force, however, had a different idea! Immediately after college graduation, I began my career in health administration as a second lieutenant in the U.S. Air Force Medical Service Corps. As I was to learn during the next 20 years (and nine moves), the needs of the Air Force always come first. I never complained, though, as those moves always produced positive experiences for my family and me. I couldn't be happier that the Air Force decided I would be a healthcare administrator. Every day brings something new to test my skills and to expand my knowledge base.

My undergraduate degree in business administration and accounting provided a solid foundation for my career in health administration. My initial education in health administration occurred during a three-month basic orientation course at Sheppard Air Force Base (AFB). I found that I was well prepared for my first assignment at the hospital at March AFB, Riverside, CA. After about two years, however, I felt that I needed additional education if I were to advance in my career. I applied for and received an Air Force Institute of Technology (AFIT) scholarship to attend graduate school at Duke University. At that time, the Duke program had an interesting introduction to the world of healthcare: new students were required to work as ward clerks in the Duke University Medical Center for three months before classes started in the fall. It was our "worm's-eye view" of the hospital. I still rely on information I learned that summer about how work gets done in healthcare. After an administrative residency at the Duke University Medical Center and Memorial Hospital in Burlington, North Carolina, I received my master of health administration (MHA) degree in 1974.

My follow-on assignment was an unaccompanied tour (no family members allowed) at Ubon Air Base in Thailand. This was very near the end of the Viet Nam War, and my job was to close the hospital and transfer all the people and equipment to other units. Although this isn't what my graduate program trained me to do, one of the things you learn as you mature is how to be flexible and how to apply the knowledge you do have to new and different situations. I completed my assignment in three months and was assigned to be administrator of a hospital in Korea to finish out my unaccompanied tour.

My next assignment was at the regional medical center at Maxwell AFB in Montgomery, Alabama. I served as squadron commander, fiscal officer, and registrar at the medical center. During this period I also served as a preceptor for master's degree students from the University of Alabama in Birmingham (UAB)—not knowing that I would eventually be a faculty member there. My next assignment was as a medical planner in the Air Force Surgeon General's Office in Europe. Our planning group changed the way the Air Force provides medical care during wartime. We established a four-echelon system of care, where the front line is trained in first aid and patients are moved from the front to the rear through progressively increasing levels of care.

While in Europe, I applied to AFIT for a scholarship that would pay for doctoral studies. I was selected and moved to Birmingham to study at UAB. I completed my Ph.D. in 1984 and was assigned to the Air Force Surgeon General's Office in Washington, D.C., to head a group of medical researchers. I retired from the U.S. Air Force in 1989, as a lieutenant colonel, and was hired by both UAB and the Birmingham Veterans' Affairs Medical Center (VAMC) as a health services researcher. Since that time I've had the best of both worlds—teaching, while keeping myself active in the practice of health administration. I currently teach courses in managed care and process improvement at UAB. At the VAMC, I am the administrative officer in surgical service.

My entire career has been in the public sector; however, in recent years, it has become very much like the private sector. We, too, are concerned with the consequences of managed care, such as utilization review, third-party billing, documentation, decreasing length-of-stay, and staffed beds.

When I entered the field everyone I knew went to work in a hospital. Now, in addition to hospitals, my students take jobs in managed care organizations, large group practices, consulting firms, and in the corporate offices of major healthcare organizations. When I received my MHA, the average student in my class was over 30 and there was only one woman in my class. Times have changed, and health administration has become a career that knows no demographic boundaries.

I think the greatest challenges for health administrators are in providing the core producers in our system—physicians—with an environment that allows them not only to produce the highest quality care in the most efficient manner, but also to do work they enjoy. Too often we make decisions without involving physicians. Physicians generally enter medicine because they want to provide a product people need without having to "sell" that product. They rely on administrative personnel to run the business side of healthcare. The challenge for us is both to include them in everything they need or want to be involved in, while protecting them from those very same issues.

My advice to someone entering the field today is to learn from everything you do. There is no bad experience. Don't think of yourself as greater than you are. Remember to practice the Golden Rule. Finally, to paraphrase futurist Joel Barker, always ask yourself, "What could I do that would radically change the way healthcare is provided today?" If you do these things, you'll have a career that is not only beneficial to society, but is fun as well. You'll never grow tired of getting up in the morning and going to work—I promise!

Sister Mary Roch Rocklage, RSM

Chairperson of the Board
Sisters of Mercy Health System
St. Louis, Missouri

R.N., St. John's School of Nursing (Missouri)
B.N., Xavier College (Illinois)
M.H.A., Saint Louis University (Missouri)
Fellow, American College of Healthcare Executives

 I AM THE chairperson of the board of directors of the Sisters of Mercy Health System—St. Louis (SMHS), which sponsors integrated delivery systems, hospitals, physician practices, and related health and human service programs throughout Arkansas, Kansas, Louisiana, Missouri, Mississippi, Oklahoma, and Texas. Before becoming the full-time chairperson in 1999, I served for thirteen years as SMHS's first president and chief executive officer. Earlier, I was director of health services and the provincial administrator for the Sisters of Mercy of St. Louis. From 1963 to 1979, I held various positions at St. John's Mercy Medical Center, including director of nursing and president.

When asked what I would do in life, I always said that I would be a nurse. I had always been involved in caring for others or organizing groups to address issues that were important to me. I have always liked to work with others and see them accomplish their desires. The transition from nursing to administration was not difficult. These roles of service are about responding to people's needs, to removing barriers so that others can function well and, to the greatest degree possible, fulfill their roles or desires. My focus has always been on working with others to pursue a common vision. I also enjoy serving others, which is the foundation of health services.

In addition to my duties with SMHS, I am adjunct professor of health care administration at Saint Louis University and at Washington University. I am also actively involved in the work of several professional associations. I am the 2001 chair-elect of the American Hospital Association; a member of the Domestic Policy Committee of the U.S. Catholic Conference; and a member of the governing boards of Wheaton Franciscan Health Services, St. Anthony's Health Services, and Alexian Brothers Health System.

The advice I would give to someone entering the health administration field is that you must truly love serving others through health services and not be overly enamored with the challenges of "corporateness." Be enthusiastic about your role of service, always remembering that administration exists only to serve those who are indispensable to health services—the women and men who provide services to one another or direct service to patients and their families. The mission of administration is to strive to assure that each encounter of service may be as effective as possible.

Terence (Terry) E. Rogers

Executive Director
St. Martin's-in-the-Pines
Birmingham, Alabama

B.S., Financial Management, University of Alabama at Birmingham

 MY CAREER HAS primarily been in home health and long-term care, with some crossover to medical temporary staffing. My responsibilities have included day-to-day operations management of branch offices of a national home health company; multi-branch oversight; consulting with hospital-based home health agencies; and selling management and information technology services to hospitals, serving as project manager for new accounts. I currently serve as executive director of a not-for-profit retirement community owned by an Episcopal foundation. Our services include independent living, assisted living, and skilled nursing care.

I entered health administration quite by accident, but I remain in the field strictly by choice. In my varying roles in health administration, there have been several consistencies—no greater responsibility exists than caring for someone's health and well-being. The stakeholders in healthcare extend beyond the actual customer or patient, staff, owners, and board members. The families, friends, and volunteers add dimensions of complexity and reward. The needs and desires of all parties create an environment in which communication and negotiation skills, compassion, financial management skills, and expertise in government regulations are absolute requirements for administrators.

Although there is no easy job in healthcare administration, the personal satisfaction in meeting community healthcare needs is great. Healthcare continues to change rapidly with regard to the payers,technology, regulation, and demographics. This dynamic environment creates never-ending opportunities for new learning and experiences.

My greatest challenges in the field have been dealing with increased regulation, increased costs to provide care, and decreased reimbursement. Expectations for quality care remain great, as does the need for financial viability and success of long term care organizations. The balance between quality and financial success is a difficult one to maintain; it requires strong leadership and motivational skills. My greatest rewards come from working with the geriatric population. In my current position, I am afforded the opportunity to know our patients and residents. My life would not be as fulfilling without these relationships and the chance to learn from their years of life.

For those interested in a career in healthcare administration, preparation and planning are vital. Healthcare administrative positions require a variety of skills, both technical and social. Strong planning, organizational, and financial skills should be acquired. Healthcare organizations face the challenge of interacting with many people; therefore, managers must have the ability to communicate with people on all levels with diverse backgrounds, cultures, and education. The ability to communicate is crucial in developing, motivating, and getting results from a large workforce.

Potential managers should begin networking in the community. Working as a volunteer in a community services organization is an effective way to learn the communication and social skills needed in healthcare. Most senior level managers and executives in healthcare start as middle managers in operations. The technical knowledge and experience gained in project management and day-to-day operations are required for effective executive leadership. Those interested in this field should seek out project management or middle management positions. As the industry continues to move forward, change will abound—and the need for management staff with planning skills and the ability to lead change will grow as well.

Peter J. Schonfeld

Senior Vice President of Policy, Health Delivery, and Data Services
Michigan Health and Hospital Association
Lansing, Michigan

B.A., Economics, Kalamazoo College (Michigan)
M.B.A., J.L. Kellogg Graduate School of Management, Northwestern
University (Illinois)

I CHOSE A healthcare career based on my interest in science and technology; in addition, several experiences during college gave me exposure to the healthcare delivery system. While an undergraduate student studying chemistry at Kalamazoo College, I entered a work-study program in a Chicago healthcare research project that required communication between trauma centers and ambulances, as well as evaluating attempts to minimize severe injuries or fatalities through better communication, education, and training. Then, as a senior, I did an individualized project for the Medical Computer Services Association in Seattle, Washington. This project investigated the feasibility and operational design of telephone electrocardiogram (EKG) services to be offered to small hospitals, physician offices, and nursing homes in the Northwest. I was a chemistry major, but through these experiences I learned that my real aptitude and motivation came from working with people—that is, management. The experiences in my work studies showed me that a career in hospital management would allow me to work with science and technology applied in healthcare settings.

With these experiences during my undergraduate studies, I decided to pursue a graduate degree in health administration and chose the master of management program at Northwestern University. While at Northwestern, I also worked part-time at Henrotin Hospital as assistant to the president. Even though this was very different from my undergraduate work, my science research background served me well in finance and business. Because it is important in administration to look at all sides of an issue and gain input from different sources before assuming a solution is evident, all the things that I had learned as a chemistry major applied.

Following graduate school, I took a position as assistant administrator at Skokie Valley Community Hospital, where my duties included managing departments and projects. I also obtained hospital risk management experience during this time and was an alternate director to Multi-Hospital Mutual Insurance, Ltd., located in Bermuda.

After my time at Skokie Valley, I returned to Henrotin Hospital in Chicago as executive vice president and chief operating officer. In this position I was responsible for managing hospital operations and for construction projects.

From Henrotin Hospital, I moved to McPherson Hospital in Howell, Michigan, where I served as president and chief executive officer for two years before taking on healthcare system responsibilities as vice president for Mission Health. In this new position, I was responsible for St. Joseph Mercy Hospital in Ann Arbor, Providence Hospital in Southfield, Salina Hospital in Saline, and McPherson Hospital in Howell.

Currently, I am senior vice president of policy, health delivery, and data services for the Michigan Health and Hospital Association. My responsibilities for the association include visioning and strategic thinking, development of delivery systems, managed care, rural healthcare, long-term care, physician-related activities, and purchaser relations. I was attracted to this position because I could work with a variety of hospitals—rural, urban, teaching, etc.—and take a much broader industry view. The opportunity to serve as an educator, consultant, and adviser on state and federal healthcare policy and regulation, while working in a smaller trade association with peers committed to improving patient access to healthcare in communities throughout Michigan, has provided great satisfaction.

In addition to my positions in hospitals, a health system, and a hospital association, I have also served as a consultant and expert witness in a variety of areas involving managed care strategies, hospital mergers, joint ventures, medical staff strategies, health insurance data management, risk management, quality assurance, and utilization review.

My greatest challenge in healthcare administration has been the search for a more successful way of providing healthcare services to all populations. Resources need to be utilized effectively to provide access and quality, while removing obstacles that prohibit people from seeking prevention and treatment programs. I believe my greatest reward has been the opportunity to help individuals and communities to improve their health, while ensuring that resources are used equitably. I have always been highly motivated to understand the needs of each area of an organization, while developing programming to meet community needs for access to healthcare services, financed by private and government purchasers.

My advice to someone entering the healthcare management profession is first to understand that everything must focus on the needs of patients, families, and communities. Get to know the people who do the work that creates and delivers healthcare. Management's purpose is to ensure that health services delivery happens with an appropriate stewardship of resources and respect for each individual. When management isn't at the office, the work still gets done; therefore, don't get caught up in the authority of management. A manager's responsibility is to serve his or her workforce. Admit what you don't know, and deliver on what you promise.

Janet Perry Stewart

Vice President, Health Information Services
Blue Cross and Blue Shield of Alabama
Birmingham, Alabama

B.S., Business Administration, University of Alabama in Huntsville
M.S.H.A., University of Alabama at Birmingham

I WAS FORTUNATE to learn about the rewards of working in healthcare before finishing elementary school. As a fifth grader, I helped my first patient. My desire to serve in the healthcare industry came from the tremendous reinforcement that I received from my early volunteer work with children with special needs and, later, from my work in basic emergency room care on Friday nights.

Because of that satisfaction, I wanted to be involved in healthcare in some way, so I sought guidance from a local hospital administrator and from the graduate program faculty in hospital and health administration at the University of Alabama at Birmingham (UAB). Those visits during my early college years convinced me that healthcare administration was the path I would pursue.

Once I chose a career, my goal became attending graduate school. During my undergraduate days at the University of Alabama in Huntsville, I did more than study. My belief was that a person in the professional arena must also be a good citizen. I served as president of the student government association, was a student member of the University of Alabama board of trustees, and served in a variety of student business and service organizations. I also volunteered and worked in for-profit, as well as not-for-profit, hospitals and clinics.

After completing my graduate school residency at the University of Alabama Hospitals, my first job was as a cost containment representative for Blue Cross and Blue Shield of Alabama. It was not the title or the salary of this position that attracted me, but the potential I believed the job and company would provide. I was not disappointed.

In 1984, then vice-president and future chief executive officer Gene Thrasher had a vision of establishing a provider network in Alabama to serve our customers better, the first statewide network of its kind. I was tapped to spearhead the development of the company's statewide Preferred Medical Doctor (PMD) program, which has evolved to become the Preferred Care Program. This program is one of the largest preferred provider organizations in the country and, is, I believe, the country's most successful. Working with this program has been one of the biggest challenges of my career—so far.

Having demonstrated my leadership skills, Blue Cross and Blue Shield of Alabama president and CEO Dick Jones asked me to develop ways to use the company's information to further benefit our customers. Because of the untapped potential of this information, the health information services division was created. After serving as vice president of managed care programs for six years, I was named the vice president of health information services (HIS), the position I currently hold. Harnessing the value of healthcare information with cutting edge technology is my current challenge.

I believe that to be successful in the healthcare industry, one must keep an open mind, be resilient, have a high energy level, and creatively embrace change. There are many rewards in my job. Hearing from our customers that we are doing a good job and hearing from doctors that they are glad their patients have Blue Cross and Blue Shield of Alabama—those are my rewards.

A more tangible reward was presented recently when Blue Cross and Blue Shield of Alabama was awarded the "DM Review World Class Solution Award for Business Intelligence: Data Warehouse Administration, Design, Management and Performance." This national award recognizes innovative, successful business intelligence implementations that provide true business value. The award can be attributed to the work my talented team has done in the HIS division.

I am an adjunct professor, mentor for students pursuing a career in healthcare, current president of Cahaba Girl Scout Council, and member of the boards of the YMCA, The Women's Committee at the Spain Rehabilitation Center, and the UAB Alumni Association. Students considering the healthcare field have to enjoy working with people and also have a heart for people. There are no limits to what you can achieve, and no limits to what you can change in the area of healthcare.

L. Clark Taylor, Jr.

President and Chief Executive Officer
Memorial Health Care System
Chattanooga, Tennessee

A.B., Economics and Biology, Transylvania University (Kentucky)
M.H.A., Virginia Commonwealth University
Ph.D., Administration of Higher Education, University of Alabama at Birmingham
Fellow, American College of Healthcare Executives

WORKING SUMMERS AS an orderly throughout high school, I discovered by accident the field of health administration. Now looking back over 30 years of working in senior administrative roles, I realize that those summers were an invaluable early preparation for a career in health administration. Understanding the patient care focus of operations at ground level is a knowledge base I often call upon. The educational route I followed was fairly traditional for the time. An undergraduate degree with a dual focus in biology and economics turned out to be a practical foundation. A master's degree in hospital administration provided the necessary advanced academic fundamentals. However, it was the administrative residency that really served as the capstone for the formal academic phase of preparation. Today fellowships are a tremendous opportunity to make the transition from school to practice, and I strongly encourage such a path.

Serving as a chief executive officer of a small hospital, as I did in my initial job after graduate school, offered a variety of first-hand experience not possible in a larger organization. My later chief executive officer experience was in academic medical centers, extremely exciting organizations combining teaching, research, and operations.

Understanding the complexity of university hospitals will prepare one for almost any organizational setting.

Health administration is a career of service to others. The richest expression is through faith-based organizations. Having been associated with health systems owned or sponsored by Baptist, United Methodist, and Roman Catholic traditions, I have seen the uniqueness of holistic care addressing mind, body, and spirit. Our medical-oriented system has been so focused on disease treatment that it has been easy to forget that health is more than the absence of disease.

In my career, there have been opportunities to teach at both the graduate and undergraduate levels. My doctoral degree has been a helpful credential in teaching, but not an essential one if the teaching is an "extracurricular" role. Teaching offers a double learning opportunity as learning occurs in preparation for teaching and again when actually engaged with students. Those in the field of health administration have many opportunities to teach, from mentoring less experienced associates to giving guest lectures in academic classes.

This brings us to the need for personal development through continuing education. Misguided is the health executive who feels mastery over the art and science of management and leadership. Learning is an attitude of curiosity, a continued evolution of skills, and the ability to be proactive in acquiring new skills.

From the research of my own doctoral dissertation came the realization that technical knowledge, as critical as it is, is not sufficient for success in health administration. Rather, interpersonal skills and the ability to develop win-win relationships are the essence of achieving things through other people. Through observing many health executives, it is clear there is much pluralism in terms of communication style, personality, and philosophy of administration. However, without relationship skills, one's career will be limited. An element of this is genuine care and respect for others. Early in my career I came across the statement that I still believe in today: "People don't care what you know, until they know that you care."

J. Larry Tyler

President
Tyler & Company
Atlanta, Georgia

B. S., Industrial Management, Georgia Institute of Technology
M.P.A., Georgia State University
Certified Public Accountant
Fellow, American Association of Healthcare Consultants
Fellow, American College of Healthcare Executives
Fellow, Healthcare Financial Management Association

 I ENTERED THE healthcare field via a non-traditional route. My undergraduate degree is from Georgia Tech in industrial management. I tried to be an engineer, but physics was my undoing. After graduating from Tech, I continued to work at the school, while getting my master's degree in accounting from Georgia State. Upon completing the degree, I joined Price Waterhouse as an auditor. Auditing was not my cup of tea, but I was determined to get my certification. I resigned the day the state board of accountancy ruled positively on my CPA application.

When I left Price Waterhouse, I went to work as the chief financial officer (CFO) for a construction company client. Later I gravitated to a fragrance manufacturer CFO position. Several years later, the search consultant who placed me in that job began to recruit me to join him and his associates in the executive search business. Because I found myself dissatisfied with the CFO job and looking to make a career change, I took a "flyer" and joined the search consultant's firm. I decided that there was a lot of upside potential and very little downside. I could always go back into public accounting if I had to, but I was fairly sure it wouldn't come to that.

Within a very short time, I was successful in the executive search business. I had found a calling. The firm had a healthcare client base, and the late 1970s were a wonderful time with a lot of business and growth. After I had been at the firm for five months, the owner of the firm decided he wanted to sell out. I bought the healthcare executive search division of the firm, which consisted of one staff person—me. Most people just leave a company and set up their own shop, but I thought there was some value in preserving the client base. I was correct.

As a search consultant, I am constantly challenged and perhaps that is why I have stayed in the business for 23 years. Because no two candidates and clients are alike, I spend my days dealing with organizations and people with their own unique circumstances. At times, the intellectual stimulation makes my head swim, and a sore throat from talking too much is an occupational hazard. I never look at the clock at the end of the day; there is still too much to do. The greatest feeling of accomplishment comes when you return to a healthcare organization years later and see how the candidate you have placed has positively affected the organization and the community. On those occasions, I can honestly say that I have made a difference.

My advice for those entering the healthcare field at this time is:

- Be flexible. Healthcare is a dynamic business that is changing daily. If you are rigid in your ways, you ought to consider some other type of business.
- Have a passion for helping others. No matter whether you are seeking a position in the for-profit or not-for-profit side of healthcare, those without compassion are eventually pushed aside. Those that do well in healthcare have a human service mentality.
- Be prepared for continuous learning because healthcare is a field where learning never ends. A master's degree is a necessity for advancement to the upper levels of the management hierarchy.

- Generally, people who like their jobs do well in them. If you find that healthcare is not your thing, don't be afraid to leave the field. Some people get caught in jobs that are not what they thought they would be and become unhappy. These people would do themselves, their families, and society a good turn by finding something to do that makes them happy. If you find a job you love, you'll never have to "work" the rest of your life.

Jane C. Udall

Senior Vice President, Clinical Operations
Legacy Health System
Portland, Oregon

B.S., Food and Nutrition, Oregon State University
M.H.A., University of Washington
Fellow, American College of Healthcare Executives

 I ENTERED THE field because I wanted to put my organization and leadership skills to work in a setting that enhanced people's health. My first college degree was in community nutrition, a choice influenced by my interest in public health and my reading of a white paper, which moved me greatly, by one of the Kennedys that described the effects of malnutrition on children on Indian reservations. After working as a public health nutritionist in Arizona for two years, I decided to pursue further education and attended the University of Washington for an MHA, which I received in 1980.

I completed a fellowship at St. Vincent Medical Center in Portland and then held several positions as a hospital administrator until my current position as a senior vice president of clinical operations at Legacy Health System. Legacy Health System is the largest Oregon-based, not-for-profit healthcare system in the state and is the sixth largest private sector employer in the four-county Portland metropolitan area. The Legacy system provides an integrated network of healthcare services, including acute and critical care, inpatient and outpatient treatment, community health education, and a variety of specialty services. In my role, I am responsible for all clinical services at four hospitals (two 100-bed suburban hospitals and two tertiary hospitals), as well as the Children's Hospital, and home health, hospice, and infusion.

Three big challenges come to mind after 21 years as a healthcare executive. One is trying to maintain a healthy home life. An understanding spouse makes it possible for an executive to commit the hours and mental energy necessary to carry out the responsibilities of the position to a high standard. A second challenge has been to work with physicians over the years as the regulatory, technology, and reimbursement environment has changed. The third challenge is the current shortage of nurses and dealing with the resulting strain on quality, patient care, nursing satisfaction, customer service, access, and cost.

The rewards have been many. During my 15-year tenure as an executive with Legacy Health System, I have influenced the philosophy, culture, and strategies of our organization. It is also rewarding to help develop new leaders from our system. The best advice I could give anyone entering the field is to remain true to your values yet flexible in your approach to leadership. Because the professional designation has been a meaningful goal for me to strive for, I have recently re-certified as a Fellow in the American College of Healthcare Executives.

Thomas B. Valuck

Vice President, External Affairs
University of Kansas Medical Center
Kansas City, Kansas

B.A., Biology, and M.D., University of Missouri–Kansas City
M.H.S.A., University of Kansas

 I HAVE NEVER considered working in a field other than healthcare. Medicine runs in my family. Growing up, all of my role models were physicians: my father and two older brothers, as well as an uncle, a cousin, and a sister-in-law. Because of the respect and gratitude I saw in the eyes of my father's patients, I knew from an early age that I wanted a career in a helping profession. Even though I have twice changed my career direction within the field, I have never regretted my decision.

Being sure of my interest in healthcare, I entered the six-year combined BA and MD program at the University of Missouri-Kansas City School of Medicine immediately after high school. Even though I was fascinated by the complexity of the basic medical sciences, I was not excited by the coursework. I was also quickly frustrated by the limitations of the one-on-one physician-patient encounter. I found myself more interested in studying the healthcare delivery system and system reform. During the first year of a pediatric residency, I decided to change my career focus and to pursue a master's degree in health services administration at the University of Kansas.

In health administration, I found the excitement that had been missing for me in clinical medicine. The idea of improving health for entire populations, reaching beyond the "microencounter" with a single patient exhilarates me. I found graduate courses in strategic planning, comparative health systems, public health, and health policy particularly interesting. I began to think, "Why limit my career impact to one clinical practice or even to an administrative position in one organization when the opportunity exists to improve the healthcare system for the whole country?"

My first job was as administrative fellow at the University of Kansas Hospital. I rotated through all the divisions of hospital management and took on several projects. Before the fellowship was complete, I was asked to take permanent employment as director of medical staff affairs. As the organization's needs changed, I advanced to an associate administrator role in operations and was then named vice president of medical affairs.

While serving in this position, I was approached by the hospital's chief executive officer and asked if I would be interested in applying for the Robert Wood Johnson Health Policy Fellowship. I had been aware of the RWJ Fellowship but never dreamed that it would be part of my future. Through the generosity of the KU Hospital and the RWJ Foundation, I was able to spend a life- and career-changing year in Washington, D.C., seeing health policy from an insider's perspective. I worked in the U.S. Senate for the Health and Education Committee, writing health policy and participating in the political process as an advisor to Senator James Jeffords, Committee Chairman.

The RWJ Health Policy Fellowship solidified my intention to focus my career toward health policy. On returning to KU Hospital, my role changed to vice president of external affairs, to incorporate my Washington experience. The role includes monitoring and influencing healthcare legislation and regulations of importance to the hospital, as well as building strategic relationships in the community.

Throughout my career, I have benefited from the insight, encouragement, and support of mentors. Kim Russel, then chief operating officer at KU Hospital, was my mentor during the administrative fellowship and first few years of my career. Kim is now CEO of Mary Greeley Medical Center in Ames, Iowa. Irene Cumming, the current chief executive officer of KU Hospital, offered me the opportunity to pursue the RWJ Fellowship and made sure that I could use the health policy experience to benefit the hospital on my return from Washington. While in Washington, Senator Jeffords and his excellent staff, including Mark Powden, Paul Harrington, Kim Monk, and Laurie Schultz-Heim ensured that my fellowship experience would be meaningful and fulfilling.

Though my career has changed direction from clinical medicine to health administration to health policy, I have continued to build experience that will be used to improve the healthcare delivery system for our country. In this rapidly changing field, it is important not only to define and work toward long-term goals, but also to be flexible and creative in the short term. I have found that healthcare is a wide-open and enormously rewarding field.

Note: Since this profile was written, Tom Valuck has left the University of Kansas Medical Center to study health law and public policy at the Georgetown University Law Center in Washington, D.C.

·

J. Philip VanLandingham,
Rear Admiral, United States Navy

Director of the Medical Service Corps/Navy Medical Inspector General
Washington, D.C.

B.S., General Management, Georgia Institute of Technology
B.B.A., Health Care Administration, Georgia State University
M.B.A., George Washington University (Washington, D.C.)
Fellow, American College of Healthcare Executives

WHEN I JOINED the Navy's Medical Service Corps, I was a student in Georgia State University's undergraduate program in healthcare administration. I had already received a bachelor of science degree in general management from the Georgia Institute of Technology, but remained uncertain as to what career field I wanted to pursue. My father and uncle had careers in the Navy, and both urged me to look toward the Medical Service Corps.

My original plan was to repay the three years I owed the Navy for the generous scholarship they had provided and to move on. After 27 years of increasingly challenging and responsible jobs in a variety of locales, I realize now that I never really seriously considered leaving. Although healthcare administration and the Navy were not originally a career calling for me, as I became exposed to the challenge of the issues, the professionalism and dedication of the people, and the satisfaction of serving our patients and country, they became my calling.

My first position with the Navy was at the National Naval Medical Center in Bethesda, Maryland. This large teaching institution exposed me to a variety of interesting jobs and laid a good foundation for the future. I then served as the aide to the Navy Surgeon General where I received a heavy dose of "the big picture" at the Navy's medical head-quarters command. In my next assignment, I was put in charge of a regional personnel support activity that primarily served the needs of the Bethesda medical staff, as well as their patient administration needs.

From there, I became a full-time graduate student, under Navy sponsorship, and earned my MBA in organizational behavior and development. After receiving my MBA, I served in Naval hospitals in Charleston, South Carolina; Guam; Orlando, Florida; Camp Lejeune, North Carolina; and Newport, Rhode Island. It was in Newport that I received the news that I had been selected to be director of the Navy's Medical Service Corps, which brought me back to Washington, and my additional assignment as Naval Medical Inspector General.

My greatest challenge also represents my greatest reward as a health services executive. The task was to merge three independently operated medical facilities, each with its own outlying clinics, into one networked organization. The goal was to reduce infrastructure with-out reducing the amount or quality of care provided. The effort was difficult, not only because of the geographic challenges, but also because of the organizational and personnel issues in merging three distinct entities into one. I was most impressed by how the leaderships at the three activities involved worked together as one to achieve the successful result—Naval Health Care New England. Their creativity, willingness to take risks, sacrifice, and focus on ensuring that the process was transparent to our patients was impressive.

My advice to a person entering health administration could be applied equally to any field of endeavor:

- Maintain a positive attitude (attitude is everything!);
- Recognize and take advantage of the power of teamwork;
- Be on time and correct in your tasks (surprisingly enough, you'll be in the minority); and
- Have fun!

Paulina Vazquez-Morris

Associate Corporate Counsel
Doctors Community Healthcare Corporation
Phoenix, Arizona

B.A., Political Science, University of Arizona
J.D., University of Arizona
M.B.A., Arizona State University
M.H.S.A., Arizona State University

AS A POLITICAL science major in college and as a student in law school, I was always interested in the socioeconomic and political aspects of healthcare. Issues such as healthcare rationing, funding choices for research or care, the growing underinsured and uninsured population, and the power dynamics of medicine all attracted my attention. More importantly, I recognized the importance of providing access to quality, affordable healthcare. I will never forget the experience of seeing a loved one whose daughter was born with a medical complication that required three of years of medical care. The astronomical bills that resulted forced this hardworking, young family into bankruptcy. It is a common story, but one which affected me profoundly.

While pursuing my bachelor's degree and my juris doctor, I gained as much exposure to health-related topics as possible through relevant classes and various political internships. As a law clerk with Kutak

Rock, a national firm, I requested health-related projects whenever possible. Following graduation from law school, I accepted a position with Kutak, and was presented with a unique opportunity. I was asked to spend the majority of my time working on-site with one of the firm's clients, a local healthcare system. This situation was the perfect opportunity for me to gain enhanced exposure to healthcare while practicing as an attorney.

During this period, I recognized my preference for working in a healthcare environment, rather than in a traditional law firm setting. I sought to make a direct contribution to healthcare and desired a stronger knowledge of health administration. After significant contemplation, I returned to school to obtain an MBA and an MHSA I pursued the dual degree after closely observing the administrators at the healthcare system and their mastery of both business and health services.

Following business school, I accepted an administrative fellowship with the Samaritan Health System (now known as Banner Health System). The fellowship was an invaluable experience and afforded me the opportunity to view the administration of a large system from the highest decision-making level. It also gave me exposure to the many positions at work within a large health system, allowing me to rule out those for which I was not well suited.

After my fellowship, I accepted a position as chief administrative counsel for the Arizona Department of Economic Security, a 10,000-employee agency that provides and/or oversees all of the social services for the state of Arizona. This was also a valuable experience, as it gave me a greater appreciation for all of the socioeconomic factors that contribute to or detract from a healthy community. I am currently employed as associate corporate counsel for Doctors Community Healthcare Corporation. This position enables me to use each of my degrees, to satisfy my interest in the law, and to tap into my passion for health services. While many challenges exist for health administrators, including the ever-changing environment, the benefits of providing one of the most important societal needs far outweigh any administrative setbacks.

My advice to those entering health services is to learn to deal with and appreciate change, experience a variety of healthcare environments, and be active in your community. Community service not only provides us with personal satisfaction, but also gives us a greater appreciation of what it takes to make a healthy community.

Katherine W. Vestal

Vice President
Health Care Consulting Services
Cap Gemini Ernst & Young U.S. LLC

B.S., Nursing, Texas Christian University
M.S., Education, Texas Woman's University
Ph.D., Allied Health Administration and Leadership, Texas A&M University
Fellow, American College of Healthcare Executives

MY CAREER IN health administration has been an amazement to me, year by year. I think I am constantly surprised and pleased by the tremendous variety of available experiences as we focus our efforts on leading healthcare into a better future. I can truthfully say that I have learned and relearned more than I ever imagined possible and have come to like the rapid pace of change and the ever-increasing requirements for health leaders.

My initial entry into healthcare was as a nurse, where I quickly found that the part of my role I liked most was management. I became a manager very early in my career and gained experience by managing units, opening a new hospital, and interfacing with all facets of the acute care setting.

It quickly became evident that to progress in the industry, I needed a master's degree to gain deeper knowledge and to have "the ticket" to advance. After my master's program, I spent several years in education, teaching at the university level. This experience made it clear that I would need a Ph.D. to advance, so I enrolled in a health administration program that provided a lot of latitude in taking courses that were related to business and leadership. From this point, I became a hospital administrator, managing various disciplines and aspects of the health network of several large teaching organizations. There is no question that I have been able to do so many interesting things because others gave me a chance to do big things early in my career. I worked very hard to succeed by being educationally prepared and by taking risks to learn new skills and to find solutions to the challenges that arose.

After 15 years in the provider business, I decided to transition to healthcare consulting and became a partner in one of the "Big Five" accounting firms. This transition allowed me to use my experiences, education, and energy in a variety of challenging client settings and to get both national and international consulting experience. I have found consulting to be an area of health administration that requires good diagnostic skills, a deep knowledge of the industry, and the stamina to travel extensively. It also requires the skills and knowledge to manage large projects and to direct the results. It is all about execution of solutions in the most complex situations.

In summary, I have had the luxury of moving back and forth among education, service, and consulting. My greatest challenges have been keeping up with the host of new knowledge and practices and working with competing agendas related to quality and costs. I think I have been well served by having personal knowledge of the complexity of actually delivering care and an understanding of the political balancing act among all of the players in the healthcare arena. I have been constantly amazed at the effect of health-related businesses, (i.e., executive search firms, suppliers, and payers) and how critical it is to network actively with others to be successful. Additionally, I have found the networks of the health associations and educational institutions to be invaluable to me.

Perhaps my message is to keep a broad perspective of the industry, think ahead to the preparation needed for your next step, contribute to the body of knowledge of health administration, and to have fun. I believe in tackling the challenges that scare you the most, mastering them, and then finding the next challenge. That is what has made for such an exciting and rewarding career for me and I think there is very little I would change if I had the chance.

Kenneth R. White

Assistant Professor and Associate Director of Professional Graduate Programs in Health Administration
Virginia Commonwealth University
Richmond, Virginia

B.S., Biology, Oral Roberts University (Oklahoma)
B.S.N., Virginia Commonwealth University
M.P.H., Health Administration, University of Oklahoma Health Sciences Center
M.S., Nursing Administration, Virginia Commonwealth University
Ph.D., Health Services Organization and Research, Virginia Commonwealth University
Fellow, American College of Healthcare Executives

 WHEN I WAS young, a new hospital opened close to my home in rural northeastern Oklahoma. Before patients were transferred to the new facility, tours were offered. Vivid in my mind are the scenes of a shiny, squeaky-clean operating room and other departments and functions that seemed so varied and full of energy. During the tour someone said, "We will run this hospital like a city within a city, with many different health professionals, support personnel, and backup resources for uninterrupted services." That was what I needed to hear to begin a dream that would launch my career as a healthcare executive.

It started with an invitation to join a medical explorer club that was headed by the local hospital administrator, Mr. B. Joe Gunn. A summer volunteer stint led to a job as an orderly in that new hospital. Fascination with hospitals and how they were organized for delivery of patient care was a newfound passion, but my career path was "semicertain." I knew that I wanted to be involved with patient care *and* running a hospital. After receiving a degree in biology, I was certain that I didn't want to make my way through more science courses. Again, I consulted my hometown mentor, Mr. Gunn, who gave me advice about graduate programs in health administration.

With a master's degree in health administration, the completion of an administrative residency at Mercy Health Center in Oklahoma City, eight years experience as an emergency department technician, and an even bigger spark to run a hospital, I was offered a job as director of planning at Mercy Health Center. During the next 14 years I assumed more responsibility in operations, including a stint as a hospital administrator for the international consulting division of the system.

This led to a turning point in my career, as I chose to return to graduate school to obtain a doctoral degree in health administration. During this time, I also completed an accelerated program in nursing. It was a homecoming, as I was living my original passion of combining knowledge of hospitals with knowledge of patient care.

My current position is with Virginia Commonwealth University as assistant professor and associate director of professional graduate programs in health administration. This is a job that is multi-faceted. For example, as a program administrator, I am responsible for admissions, student activities, curriculum planning, and administrative residency and job placement. As a teacher, I have responsibility for designing and conducting classes that meet the needs of students from diverse backgrounds. As a researcher, I am contributing new knowledge to the field of health administration.

My research interests are centered in two areas, the role and services of church-owned hospitals and the future of the nursing and health administration professions. Service to the community is important, too. This is carried out as a board member of a health system and as a volunteer for an inner-city clinic that serves persons who are uninsured.

The greatest challenges have been in providing quality patient care with a quality workforce, with scarce resources. The greatest rewards of my career have been serving others, knowing that I have made a difference in the life of another person, as a mentor, teacher, scholar, or nurse. A piece of advice that I have for someone entering health administration is this, "Never forget that the patient is the reason we exist. Learn all you can about the business side of healthcare *and* the perspective of the patient."

Note: Since this profile was written, Kenneth White has been promoted to associate professor and director of the MHA *program at Virginia Commonwealth University.*

Gorie Williams, Jr.

Research Administrator, Mayo Clinic
Rochester, Minnesota

B.S., Chemistry, Angelo State University, San Angelo, Texas
M.B.A., Arizona State University
M.H.S.A., Arizona State University

MY INTEREST IN health administration began when my career as an environmental chemist was not going in the direction I wanted. I came to the conclusion that I wanted to be in a position where I could influence change for the betterment of society as a whole, or at least of my community.

Having a nurse as a mother, I had known at an early age that I wanted to be involved in the healthcare field in some capacity. Observing the way she catered to and cared for her patients amazed me. Likewise, knowing the morbidity and mortality that we face as a society made it more apparent that, since I consider myself a "generalist," health administration was where I belonged. After taking a few graduate courses in health administration at a nearby university, I knew that this was the avenue that would enable me to make a positive impact in the community in which I live and the institution I serve.

After these initial courses, I decided to enroll full time in the health administration program at Arizona State University. My educational preparation included courses in the MBA program (e.g., finance, accounting, marketing, organizational behavior, economics, and statistics), plus health administration courses (e.g., health economics, health organizational structure, managed care, long-term care, health finance, outcomes research, epidemiology, health law).

My current position is research administrator. I facilitate grant, finance, and personnel administration for community medicine, psychiatry and psychology, pulmonary and critical care medicine, and health sciences research (biostatistics, epidemiology, medical information resources, health services education, and survey research).

I am currently in the process of determining what path my career will follow, as the institution where I am employed offers many opportunities. I have made it to "administrator" status, and I am concentrating on what it means and takes to be an administrator. However, I would like for my career path to stay in operations, linked to the community because the community is the basis of healthcare. To achieve this, I plan to volunteer on community boards.

My greatest challenge as a health services executive is figuring out all the nuances of what it takes to be an effective and efficient leader. Just when I think I understand, something comes along and changes the way I view things. My greatest reward is helping my departments achieve their goals and being able to pave the way for them.

The best advice I can give to someone entering the health administration field is to seek out a mentor who will help you through the rough spots, as well as the smooth. Most of all, know your staff and always be there to help and support them in any situation.

Robert J. Zasa

Partner
Woodrum Ambulatory Systems Development
Pasadena, California

B. A., English, University of Alabama at Tuscaloosa
M.S.H.H.A., University of Alabama at Birmingham
Fellow, American College of Medical Practice Executives

 I BEGAN MY career in healthcare in the housekeeping department of Baptist Medical Centers of Birmingham, Alabama. During my senior year at the University of Alabama, I was an administrative clerk at Druid City Hospital in Tuscaloosa, where I enjoyed the mentorship of D. O. McCloskey. After graduating from Alabama, I moved to the University of Alabama at Birmingham (UAB), where I completed a master's of science in hospital and health administration, doing my administrative residency at the Ochsner Clinic in New Orleans. As a graduate student, I had excellent mentors in Edgar J. Saux, Francis Manning, L. R. Jordan, and Austin Letson. It was Mr. Jordan who gave me my first job, and Mr. Letson exposed me to all aspects of the hospital.

Later, I would become associate administrator of Brookwood Hospital in Birmingham. Because I had experience in opening new ambulatory care services and a satellite clinic for Ochsner Clinic, I was assigned to develop a 140,000 square foot ambulatory care center on the Brookwood campus and eight satellite clinics at some distance from the hospital. I was acting chief operating officer of Brookwood in 1981, the year after American Medical International (AMI), a predecessor of Tenet Corporation, acquired Brookwood. Later, I became vice president and chief operating officer of AMI's subsidiary, AMI Ambulatory Centers, Inc., at its headquarters office in California.

It was during my tenure at Brookwood that I returned to school. I took classes at Loyola University of New Orleans and at Birmingham Southern College. I also completed an executive certificate in medical marketing at the UCLA School of Public Health and received my fellowship from the American College of Medical Practice Executives.

In 1983, I left AMI and joined a group of physicians who wanted to consolidate their ambulatory surgery centers. That group became Alternacare Corporation, with which I stayed until its acquisition by Columbia Health Care in 1986. That year, I formed my own national ambulatory care consulting firm, Ambulatory Systems Development Corporation. With offices in Nashville, Tennessee, and Pasadena, California, my firm provided feasibility, development, and management services to ambulatory surgery centers throughout the United States. Later, with venture capital backing, I formed Premier Ambulatory Systems, serving as its chief executive officer. In 1995 and 1996, *Inc.* magazine recognized me as chief executive officer of one of the 500 fastest-growing companies in the United States.

In 1997, I sold Premier to HealthSouth, Inc., and, with David Woodrum and Joseph Zasa, formed Woodrum/Ambulatory Systems Development, managing and owning minority shares in surgery centers nationwide. I teach in both UCLA's and UAB's graduate and executive programs in health administration. I have written many articles for healthcare publications, have contributed to chapters of two textbooks, and serve on the editorial board of three periodicals.

My greatest professional challenges and rewards have been in learning how to understand and relate to physicians, to work together in a team. I love working with physicians and it is rewarding to hear how much they appreciate my understanding of them.

My advice to someone entering the field is to work to understand physicians and the needs of the many players in healthcare. The "art" of managing people and motivating them is the best skill set that one can develop. A healthcare executive needs to complement this skill set with a very keen understanding of how to manage a business financially, how to make a budget really happen, and how to adapt to changing circumstances to adjust politically and to win financially. These are key skill sets to develop, and are critical for future healthcare executives to succeed for their organizations and themselves.

Appendix

ORGANIZATIONAL RESOURCES FOR EXPLORING
CAREERS IN HEALTHCARE MANAGEMENT

Accrediting and Academic Organizations

AACSB—The International Association for Management Education
600 Emerson Road, Suite 300
St. Louis, Missouri 63141–6762
314-872-8481
http://www.aacsb.edu

AACSB—The International Association for Management education is a not-for-profit corporation of educational institutions, corporations, and other organizations devoted to the promotion and improvement of higher education in business administration and management. AACSB is the premier accrediting agency for bachelor's, master's, and doctoral degree programs in business administration and accounting.

Accrediting Commission on Education for Health Services Administration
730 Eleventh Street, NW, Suite 400
Washington, D.C. 20001–4510
202–638-5131
http://www.acehsa.org

The Accrediting Commission on Education for Health Services Administration (ACEHSA) is a group of educational, professional, and commercial organizations devoted to accountability and quality improvement in the education of health administration professionals. ACEHSA is the accrediting body for master's programs in health administration.

Association of University Programs in Health Administration
730 Eleventh Street, NW, Fourth Floor
Washington, D.C. 20001–4510
202–638-1448
http://www.aupha.org

The Association of University Programs in Health Administration (AUPHA) is a not-for-profit association of university-based educational programs, leading executives, and provider organizations with an interest in the development and continuous improvement of management education.

Council on Education for Public Health
800 Eye Street, NW, Suite 202
Washington, D.C. 20001–3710
202–789-1050
http://www.ceph.org

The Council on Education for Public Health (CEPH) accredits schools of public health and certain public health programs offered in settings other than schools of public health.

Professional Organizations

American Association of Healthcare Consultants
1926 Waukegan Road, Suite 1
Glenview, Illinois 60025
847–657-6964
http://www.aahc.net

The American Association of Healthcare Consultants (AAHC) is a not-for-profit organization that is as a credentialing body for consultants practicing is all areas of healthcare organization and delivery.

American College of Health Care Administrators
1800 Diagonal Road, Suite 355
Alexandria, Virginia 22314
703–739-7900; 888–88-ACHCA (toll-free)
http://www.achca.org

The American College of Health Care Administrators (ASCHA) provides professional development and educational opportunities to long-term care administrators to improve the quality of care for those they serve.

American College of Healthcare Executives
Suite 1700
One North Franklin Street
Chicago, Illinois 60606–3491
312–424-2800
http://www.ache.org

The American College of Healthcare Executives (ACHE) is an international professional society of nearly 30,000 healthcare executives. It is known for its prestigious credentialing and continuing education programs. ACHE works toward its goal of improving the health status of society by advancing healthcare leadership and management excellence.

American College of Physician Executives
4890 West Kennedy Boulevard, Suite 200
Tampa, Florida 33609
813–287-2000; 800–562-8088 (toll-free)
http://www.acpe.org

The American College of Physician Executives (ACPE) is a membership organization for physician executives with management or administrative responsibilities in hospitals, group practices, managed care, government, universities, the military, and industry. ACPE provides a number of educational programs and a certification process for its members.

American Organization of Nurse Executives
One North Franklin
Chicago, Illinois 60606
312–422-2800
http://www.aone.org

The American Organization of Nurse Executives (AONE), a subsidiary of the American Hospital Association, is a national organization of nurses who design, facilitate, and manage care. The organization provides leadership, professional development, advocacy, and research to advance nursing practice and patient care, promote nursing leadership excellence, and shape healthcare public policy.

American Public Health Association
800 Eye Street, NW
Washington, D.C. 20001–3710
202–777-2742
http://www.apha.org

The American Public Health Association (APHA) is an organization of public health professionals. APHA and its members seek to influence policies and set priorities for public health.

American Society for Healthcare Human Resources Administration
One North Franklin
Chicago, Illinois 60606
312–422-3725
http://www.ashhra.org

The American Society for Healthcare Human Resources Administration (ASHHRA), a subsidiary of the American Hospital Association, is an organization of human resources professionals who work in healthcare organizations. Its mission is to advance excellence and increase competency in human resources management within healthcare organizations.

Association of Hispanic Healthcare Executives
c/o Sun Health Boswell Memorial Hospital
Attention: George Perez
10401 Thunderbird Boulevard
Sun City, Arizona 85351
602–876-5356

The Association of Hispanic Healthcare Executives (AHHE) promotes the availability and development of healthcare executives dedicated to enhancing the quality of and access to healthcare for the Hispanic community in the United States. AHHE provides networking opportunities for members, maintains a national resume bank, and supports a mentoring program.

Healthcare Financial Management Association
Two Westbrook Corporate Center, Suite 700
Westchester, Illinois 60154–5700
800–252-HFMA (toll-free)
http://www.hfma.org

The Healthcare Financial Management Association (HFMA) is a professional membership organization for financial management professionals employed in healthcare organizations. HFMA helps members by providing professional development and certification opportunities, networking, and communicating information and technical data.

Healthcare Information Management and Systems Society
230 East Ohio Street. Suite 500
Chicago, Illinois 60611–3269
312–664-4467
http://www.himss.org

The Healthcare Information Management and Systems Society (HIMSS) is a not-for-profit organization representing information and management systems professional in healthcare, serving its members by providing leadership, education, and networking.

Institute for Diversity in Health Management
One North Franklin, Thirtieth Floor
Chicago, Illinois 60606
312–422-268; 800–233-0996 (toll-free)
http://www.DiversityConnection.org

The Institute for Diversity in Health Management is committed to expanding opportunities for healthcare leadership for ethnic minorities and increasing the number of qualified minorities in health services management positions. The Institute offers a Summer Enrichment Program, a Fellowship Program, and a Scholarship Program.

Medical Group Management Association
104 Inverness Terrace East
Englewood, Colorado 80112–5306
303–799-1111; 877–275-6462 (toll-free)
http://www.mgma.org

The Medical Group Management Association (MGMA) represents medical group practice in the U.S. Its purpose is to improve the effectiveness of medical group practices and the knowledge and skills of the individuals who manage and lead them. The American College of Medical Practice Executives (ACMPE) is MGMA's professional development and credentialing arm.

National Association of Health Services Executives
8630 Fenton Street, Suite 126
Silver Spring, Maryland 20910
202–628-3953
http://www.nahse.org

The National Association of Health Services Executives (NAHSE) is a not-for-profit association of black healthcare executives. Its purpose is to promote the advancement and development of black healthcare leaders and to elevate the quality of healthcare services rendered to minority and underserved communities.

Cynthia Carter Haddock

Professor and Chair
Department of Health Policy and Management
University of Kansas Medical Center
Kansas City, Kansas

B.S., Mathematics, Missouri Southern State College
M.A., Statistics, University of Missouri–Columbia
Ph.D., Medical Care Organization and Administration, Cornell University
(New York)

 Professor Haddock began her career in health administration as a data analyst in a health planning agency in mid-Missouri. Since completing her Ph.D., she has held faculty appointments at Saint Louis University, the University of Alabama at Birmingham, the University of Colorado at Denver, and the University of Kansas Medical Center.

Professor Haddock has taught courses in organization theory and behavior, human resources management, and health policy. She has served as a faculty member for workshops in Armenia (1997) and Bosnia-Herzegovina (1998) and led a partnership with an educational program in Armenia (1999–2001). Her research interests are in health policy and human resources management, and she is currently research director of a study of the uninsured in Kansas.

Professor Haddock has published numerous articles in health services journals. She has served as on the editorial boards of *Medical Care Review* and *Frontiers in Health Services Management,* and she is currently a member of the editorial boards of *Healthcare Papers* (a Canadian journal), the *Journal of Healthcare Management,* and the *Journal of Health and Human Services Administration.* She has held a number of leadership positions in national professional associations. She is a past chair of the Health Care Administration Division of the Academy of Management and a past chair of the board of directors of the Association of University Programs in Health Administration. She has served as a Fellow of the Accrediting Commission on Education for Health Services Administration and continues to be a site visitor for the Commission. Professor Haddock is a member of the Academy for Health Services Research and Policy and a faculty associate of the American College of Healthcare Executives.

During the 1994–1995 academic year, Professor Haddock was a Robert Wood Johnson Health Policy Fellow. As an RWJ Fellow, she worked on healthcare issues in the Office of the Senate Democratic Leader Thomas A. Daschle (D-SD).

Robert A. McLean

Professor and Director
Master of Health Services Administration Program
Creighton University
Omaha, Nebraska

B.A., Economics, University of Texas at Austin
M.A., Economics, University of Texas at Austin
Ph.D., Labor Economics, Cornell University (New York)
Chartered Financial Analyst

PROFESSOR MCLEAN BEGAN his career in health economics and finance as a research associate in the American Medical Association's Center for Health Services Research and Development in 1978. He taught in the health administration programs of the University of Kansas, the University of North Carolina at Chapel Hill, and the University of Alabama at Birmingham before joining Creighton University in 1999.

In addition to his textbook, *Financial Management in Healthcare Organizations* (ITP/Delmar, second edition, forthcoming), he has published articles in the *American Journal of Public Health*, the *Health Care Management Review*, *Health Services Research*, *Health Services Management Research*, *Hospital and Health Services Administration*, and other journals. His research focuses on the application of options theory to the decisions of healthcare organizations.

Professor McLean has been active in the development of health administration education programs. A Fulbright lecturer at the Czech Republic's Palacký University (1997) and a member of the Public Health faculty of the American University of Armenia, he has taught in workshops in Bosnia-Herzegovina and Ukraine. He has also been a consultant to the Commission on Academic Accreditation, Ministry of Higher Education and Research, United Arab Eminates.

Professor McLean is a member of the Nebraska chapter of the Healthcare Financial Management Association and is a faculty associate of the American College of Healthcare Executives. He served on the finance committee of the Association of University Programs in Health Administration (1998–2001) and was an associate editor of *Business Library Review International* from 1998 until the suspension of its publication in 2001.

Robert C. Chapman

President and Chief Executive Officer
Eastern Health System, Inc.
Birmingham, Alabama

B.S., Chemistry, Alabama College (University of Montevallo)
M.S.H.H.A., University of Alabama at Birmingham
Fellow, American College of Healthcare Executives

MR. CHAPMAN WORKED as an application research chemist for Monsanto Textiles Division in Decatur, Alabama, prior to beginning his career in health services administration in 1970 as an administrative clerk at East End Memorial Hospital in Birmingham, Alabama. Following the completion of the academic requirements and a one-year residency at East End Memorial Hospital, he received a master of science in hospital and health administration from UAB in 1972. He quickly rose through the leadership ranks to become executive vice president and chief executive officer of East End Memorial Hospital and Health Centers in 1975. Following the 1985 reorganization of East End Memorial Association, he was appointed president and chief executive officer of Eastern Health System, Inc, a regional integrated healthcare delivery system.

Mr. Chapman has held an academic appointment with UAB since 1976 and is an adjunct professor in the master of science in health administration program. He has mentored over 30 residents. He has also held academic appointments with the University of Alabama and The George Washington University. In addition to teaching, his organization is a sponsor of the Institute for Diversity on Health Management's

Summer Enrichment Program, providing opportunities for minority students to explore careers in health services administration. He has published an article in *Medical-Surgical Review*.

Mr. Chapman's contributions to health administration have been many, including service on the boards of directors for many organizations such as the American Hospital Association and Blue Cross Blue Shield of Alabama. He has also served on the State of Alabama Department of Public Health Licensure Advisory Board.

Mr. Chapman is a Fellow in the American College of Healthcare Executives and has served two terms on the ACHE Council of Regents as regent for Alabama. He is also a member of the National League for Nursing and the Alabama League for Nursing.

MORE CAREER RESOURCES FROM HEALTH ADMINISTRATION PRESS

A Career Guide for the Health Services Manager, Third Edition
Anthony R. Kovner, Ph.D., and Alan H. Channing, FACHE

Learn the professional and personal skills necessary to succeed as a healthcare executive. This book covers everything from finding your career niche to working with clinicians.

Topics covered include:
- Where health services managers work
- How to build an ideal career
- What skills make a good manager
- How to manage physicians, boards, and other employees
- How to advance within an organization and within the industry

Order No. BKCO-1078, $43 + shipping
Softbound, 203 pp, 2000
ISBN 1-56793-111-1
An ACHE Management Series Book

Tyler's Guide
The Healthcare Executive's Job Search, Third Edition
J. Larry Tyler, FACHE, FAAHC

If you are considering a job search in the competitive healthcare management market, this book is a must read. Recruitment expert Larry Tyler presents sample correspondence, sample interview questions, excellent tips for networking, and suggestions for preparing an eye-catching resume. This new edition includes updated chapters on using search consultants and the Internet for job searching, making the transition from student to professional, and list of helpful web resources.

Expert advice on:
- Getting motivated
- Building and maintaining a network of colleagues
- Crafting resumes and cover letters
- Using the Internet in your job search
- Dealing with interviews and follow-up
- Making the transition from the military
- Making the transition from student to professional
- Overcoming discrimination
- Evaluating job offers

Order No. BKCO-1148, $50 + shipping
Softbound, 244 pp, March 2002
ISBN 1-56793-178-2
An ACHE Management Series Book

Order these books by phone at (301) 362-6905 or online at www.ache.org/hap.cfm

Prices are subject to change.